A Boy's Sex Life

A Boy's Sex Life

**A HANDBOOK OF BASIC INFORMATION
AND MORAL GUIDANCE**

William J. Bausch

Fides/Claretian
Notre Dame, Indiana 46556

Library of Congress Card Number: 78-93236
SBN:8190-0520-7
6773

To My Parents

who taught without words

Contents

Introduction for Adults

Boys are sexual beings. They are and can never be otherwise. One of the illusions of the adult world (especially the world of parents) is to deny this fact of life in practice. Yet the boy is sexed and his attitudes about sex are formed very early. Often as not he is given negative attitudes by his parents. Disgusted looks, dire warnings, expressions of "shame" and "dirty" or just simple silence about sex give a negative education about it. The result is that the average boy's sex education is left to the streets and the magazines and the TV set. By the time the boy reaches pubescence and strong emotions are upheaving throughout his mind and body he has few facts to help him interpret his new adolescent role and much nonsense masquerading as fact to hinder him. Yet, fact or fiction, the new emotions are there. He *does* have a sex life. He is now subject to stimulation. He is drawn to girls, feels curiosity about other boys, wonders about his "bad" thoughts, is frightened by his erections and embarrassed by his wet dreams. And he has no one to ask.

The Catholic boy will be concerned about sin, of course. His going to communion will diminish. He is torn between the traditional taboos about sex and the openness and outright seduction of the society about him. There are certain commandments "against" sex but he has confession to fall back on if he fails. In middle adolescence, however, unless he comes to better terms with himself and with his religion, he is apt, except on occasion, to forsake both the "repressive" commandments and going to confession. He sees the former as unrealistic and the latter as meaningless since he knows he'll "do it again."

We spoke of the outright seduction of society. There is no doubt that more than ever boys have mixed feelings about sex as a result of this seduction. They are sometimes really overwhelmed by the frankness and excesses they witness today. They are being shaped by the mass media where the only time the average American boy witnesses signs of affection or two people kissing one another passionately or embracing is among the unmarried. They all know of one or two of their friends whose parents are separated or divorced. Natural sex interest gets forced by little fifth and sixth grade girls who run around in net stockings, mini skirts and falsies. At times he finds himself on the dance floor instead of the basketball court. He reads about the "nude-ins" at demonstrations. He's heard of the plays on Broadway where both actors and audience take off their clothes. Provocative sex lurks on every paperback cover and *Playboy* pictures are passed around in any school, public or parochial. More and more he is exposed to "uni-sex" with boys in girls clothing and girls wearing boys clothing. Homosexuality is becoming more the "in" thing and jokes on perversion are not uncommon among grammar school children. In short, there is simply no discernable context into which to place the average boy's sex education. Confusion so prevalent, innocence so soon tarnished make one pause. It makes one want to write a book like this.

There are, of course, several good books about sex that a boy could read. Some are excellent and written from a christian point of view. The Lutheran Concordia Series on sex education, for instance, is quite adequate. Others are either too moralistic, too naturalistic or outright pagan and against every Jewish-Christian tradition known. There is nothing as such that is written for the Catholic boy within the framework of his daily life and his religious practices. This book is written for him.

But this is not quite accurate. It is really written for a larger audience than the average Catholic boy—or, I should say, for a more supportative audience. For this is a book whose language and style frequently bypass the average boy. This is partly because certain subjects need more precision than "watering down" will afford. More importantly, however, this is because all books on the sensitive subject of sex need guidance and further explanation. This guidance and explanation should come from an adult—a parent, a teacher, a clergyman. This book, therefore, is written for adults and moral counselors of the adolescent boy. Ideally, the most effective use of this book would be to have it read under the supervision of a counseling adult rather than just by the boy himself.

This book is the result of over a dozen years of sex education for boys. As an acknowledged cliché, they have taught me many times. My experiences with them over the years have been rewarding and at times rejoiceful. I remember the boy who, with great relief, confided to me that he thought he was sick and was happy to learn that erections were quite normal. The "late bloomers" were reassured when they learned that they would catch up with their buddies; it was just a matter of their "alarm clock" (pituitary gland) going off. Fears concerning undersized sexual organs and feelings of homosexuality have been put to rest. Most of all, the experience of sheer sexual joy is a great discovery. We talk about that in the chapter of that name.

In this small book I have tried to rework traditional morality with modern insights of psychology and religious education. Some may find my morality too liberal and my psychology too conservative. Others will be taken aback, I am sure, by the bluntness of the language or the directness of the tone. It has been my experience with boys, however, that the direct approach is appreciated as long as genuine vulgarity is avoided and there is an attitude, a tone of respect in the background.

I wish to thank Claretian Publications for permission to reprint the chapters on masturbation. Also I am indebted to the insights of Dr. Peter Bertocci in the chapter on "Sex; Discharge or Symbol" and to the thoughtful ideas of Robert O'Neil and Michael Donovan about "bad thoughts" and fantasies in the chapter, "Sexual Joy." The rest of the material, as I have indicated, is the compilation of teaching and experience over the years. More than I realize much of this book is derivative but the sources are lost to the conscious awareness or the conscious memory. Finally, I wish to thank Miss Ann DeVizia who carefully and patiently typed the manuscript.

CHAPTER I

The Male Vocation

INTRODUCTION

Jimmy and Jean are six years old in the first grade. Like all of their classmates they have, for all practical purposes, and to the untrained eye, the same height, weight, shape, size and build. In fact, if their parents let Jimmy's hair grow long and put pants on Jean you couldn't tell them apart. Why do these kids in the first, second, third grades, etc. have the same size, appearance, shape and height so you can't tell them apart? Or, put it this way: if you waited and took a look at Jimmy and Jean when they're in the seventh, eighth and ninth grades on up, there will be no trouble telling the male from the female. Why? Why are the body structures of Jimmy and Jean so alike when in the first grade and so different in the eighth? Think about it. To jar your imagination into thinking, picture this. You're in class in school when a knock comes at the door. It's a kid from the second grade delivering a message to the teacher. Imagine your double-take when he comes inside the room: this second grader has broad shoulders and big muscles, sporting a moustache yet and saying, "Here's a message for you, teacher" in a deep baritone voice!

Well, you may smile at this, but it raises the point of why you would find a little boy with the build of a man so funny. It brings up again our question of why boys and girls are almost the same in the lower grades so that, outside of their sexual organs, you can't tell them apart and yet they are so different in the upper grades and thereafter. In fact, to answer these questions we must raise another: why Jimmy and Jean at all? why boys and girls? why *two* sexes?

The answer is as simple as the everyday fact that when you do work at home or around school you automatically and sensibly choose the right tool for the job. You don't write with a ruler and don't measure with a pen. You don't hammer with plyers and don't cut wire with a hammer. You select the right tool for the right job. You know that before these tools were invented some engineers sat down around a drawing board and the first and obvious question they asked was, "What is it *for?* What do we want to achieve?" Someone says, "Well, there's this thing called a nail sticking out of a piece of wood and somebody's going to want to get it out of there, so let's design a tool that will do the job." In due time the engineers come up with a claw hammer. Not a screwdriver, notice, but a hammer. They fitted the tool to the job.

If we know anything about God we know that He is the greatest engineer of them all. In the world of nature, He looks at the job to be done and fits the tool to it. All the marvelous adaptations of nature are proofs of this from the claws of the lion to the radar of the bat. He gives all of nature a job and provides the tools to carry it out. In the general running of our planet God follows the same rule. The world is here for a purpose and He put two human beings in charge of carrying out this purpose. He gave each of them a special function or vocation so that, together, they would bring about achievement. One of these beings would be a warrior, bridge builder, defender of the home, athlete, maker of spacecraft and provider. The other would be maker of the home, bearer of children, geared for the details of life. With two such complementary purposes it was only natural that God should invent two different "tools" two sexes, a man and a woman. They would be "tooled" to do their different jobs and both together they would help each other and supply both physically and emotionally what the other lacked.

Now, of course, running a world is pretty big business and should be entrusted to responsible people. Children, by definition, are irresponsible and immature. They're supposed to be. Someone takes care of them. These little kids in the first grade—why, look at the care they get from adults, especially their parents. Mommy gets them up in the morning, washes them, dresses them, feeds them and sends them off to school. When these kids come home, Mommy's there to take care of them. They come to the table and eat the food that Daddy provided for them. They turn on lights whose electricity they are not paying for; they watch a TV set that someone else bought. In short, they live in a world of being taken care of, of adult care and help. That's why the kids in the lower grades look the same. There's no need to be different. There's no need for adult equipment to do a job. They *are* part of the job. Someone still is taking care of them!

But, of course, this cannot continue forever. Someday Mommy and Daddy will get older and finally die. Someone has to step into their shoes of responsibility. To bring this about, God has provided a transition period in the lives of children called 'adolescence,' a time period dur-

ing which the irresponsible body of the child gives way to
the responsible body of the adult. For you Latin brains
the whole story is told in the principle parts of the Latin
verb *adolesco*. They are: *adolesco, adolescere, adultus*
(its a deponent verb). It means "to grow up." I only
mention this because you can see that the past participle
of "to grow up" is "having grown up" or *adultus* from
which we get our word "adult." An adult is one who has
grown up both physically, emotionally and spiritually. A
child is one who has not. An adolescent (teenager we
say) is one who is passing from childhood to adulthood.
So we come to this definition of adolescence: *Adolescence is the process by which a boy and girl leave the
neutral state of childhood and assume the physical and
mental structure of adult life.* Let's take a look at this interesting process. We'll start with you, the boy.

*   *   *

We must begin with a little science. Dotted around the
human body are little chemical manufacturing plants
called glands. These glands manufacture chemicals or
hormones which regulate normal size and growth. If the
right combination and flow of these hormones are not
produced you will get abnormality. Many of your circus
freaks have glandular problems. The seventeen foot
giant, the 680 pound fat lady, the dwarf, all probably
have some glandular defect that caused or contributed to
their condition. Of the many glands in the body the two
glands we're interested in at the moment are the pituitary
gland at the base of the brain and the sex glands in the
lower trunk of the body (Figure 1). The pituitary gland

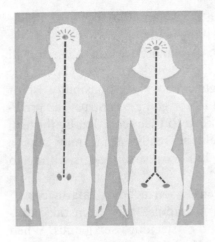

FIGURE I

is very important because, although no larger than the tip of your fingernail, it does reside in your "computer," your brain. As such, it's the master gland regulating all the others. Other glands operations depend on signals from this gland. In relationship to the sex glands we can speak of the pituitary gland as an "alarm clock"; that is, it is programmed to "ring" at a certain time and so "wake up" the sleeping sex glands. Every boy, of course, is born with sex glands, but, for all practical purposes they do not work. They are "asleep." They go to work when awakened by the pituitary gland. Generally for most boys this "alarm clock" goes off at the end of seventh or during eighth grade. But for some it goes off earlier, others later. This explains how come boys in the eighth grade, for example, both of whom may be thirteen years old and one guy is big and hairy and the other guy looks like a fifth grader. It's just a difference in their programming controlled by the pituitary gland. Whether you're among the early starters or late starters, don't worry. Your "alarm clock" will even things out.

Getting back to the sex glands, we said that, for all practical purposes, they don't work for young boys. The reason is the one we gave above: responsibility is for adults, not kids, so God is not going to entrust the growing up powers of sex to kids. But He feels that by thirteen or fourteen a boy should be ready. Some may not be ready for responsibility but most are. God is willing to take the risk.

All right, what happens when a boy's "alarm clock" goes off? Well, a chemical impulse goes from this pituitary gland and wakes up the "sleeping" sex glands. When this happens, watch out! For the next four or five years there will be a rapid development as your body gets fitted out for adult living and adult responsibility. Now in order to appreciate what happens, let's take a look at the boy's sexual organs and learn the technical terms.

As you can see from Figure 2, there are three parts to

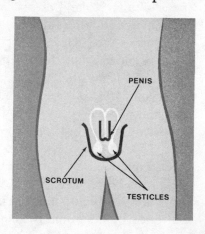

FIGURE 2

a boy's sexual organs. There are the *testicles* or testes. These are the sex glands themselves, the ones that awakened by the pituitary gland will produce the chemicals that will enable a boy to grow up. Around the testicles is a thick covering of skin called the *scrotum*. This has two purposes. One is to protect the testicles from being hurt or damaged. Damage done to a growing boy's testicles may keep him from growing up at all. These testicles are tender, like two small almonds (hence the slang "balls," or "nuts" that some kids call the testicles, mostly, I suspect, because they don't know the real terms). You know the testicles are tender if you ever got hit between the legs by a ball or something. It really hurt! Secondly, for the testicles to function properly they must have a proper temperature and here is something that you have experienced: when you are swimming and the water's cold, notice how the scrotum wrinkles up as it were and tightens the testicles against your body. It is lifting them closer to your main body to get your body heat. On the other hand, when you're very hot and it's warm outside, your scrotum will stretch downward there-by lowering your testicles away from too much body heat. The final part of a boy's sexual organs is the *penis*, the finger-like part. This penis has two purposes also. One is that this is the part from which a boy urinates: his liquid waste empties out through the penis. The other purpose of the penis is that of contact; it is his "contact" organ that will join him to a woman someday. So, these are the parts of a boy's sexual organs: the *testicles*, the *scrotum* and the *penis*. The general size of a boy's sexual organs, by the way, has nothing to do whatever with their function any more than the size of an eye affects seeing or the size of a nose affects smelling. Having large, medium or small sex organs is like having a large, medium or small nose.

Now let us see what happens when the pituitary gland kicks off the sex glands and starts them working. First, we might mention that hair begins to grow around the sexual organs. It is usually several shades darker than the hair on your head and is coarse. For most boys this hair, called *pubic hair,* will be the first outward sign that their "alarm clock" has gone off. Over the years it will multiply and grow roughly in a triangular shape from the base of his penis up the navel (belly button). Other hair will grow on his calfs, under his arms, thighs, etc. But there are other dramatic changes for a boy. His baby fat begins to melt into muscle. His sexual organs themselves grow two or three times larger—an obvious necessity since they are going to have such an important part to play in his development. His bones which have a slight separation between them begin to knit together and "lock." A boy's skeleton is on the way to becoming something like a one-welded car frame: it can stand stress and strain better. The boy-becoming-a-man is going to need a solid frame to withstand hard work and stress. That's why, by the way, coaches don't want a kid under sixteen to play football without the proper equipment. He's too easy a target for a bone break or a ligament tear.

Under the force of the new chemicals pumping into him from his sex glands a boy grows taller. He'll probably grow more in the next three years than he's grown in the first ten or twelve. And, of course, to feed all those multiplying cells! No wonder parents can't keep the refrigerator full. They have a food-eating teenage monster on their hands! A boy at this time begins to sprout hair on his upper lip and shaving may be just around the corner. His voice which was as high as a girl's voice, begins to descend to the register of a man's voice. It's amusing to me when I go into the eighth grade and say, "Good morning." You should hear all the cracked "good mornings" I get back. Voices are hitting the high notes and the low notes in one word.

At this time a boy's oil glands begin to operate too. Before when he was hot he could perspire. Now he sweats and can have BO. His oil glands now can produce the oil that mixes with bacteria and cause odor. Pimples on the face can be a problem too at this time because the chemical reactions can be too rapid and so bring this condition on. On the other hand, dirt may lodge in the pores of the skin. The oil's trying to ooze out and meeting this obstacle can result in those white or black heads. Washing one's face often with a mild soap and not over eating the greasy foods or sweets will help to make this condition temporary. Sometimes, too, during the beginning of adolescence a boy's breasts can become sensitive and maybe he'll even feel a hard little knot beneath the nipple. If this happens, let it alone. This is temporary and will go away in a short time.

Notice, now, how really important the sex organs are and how vital their function. If a boy's sexual organs did not work properly he would never grow taller, his bones would never knit, his muscles would not develop, he would never need a shave, his voice would always be high pitched, he would never really have the appearance of a man (Figure 3). Sex, you see, is a very big concept. It involves all of a boy, his whole physical and emotional framework.

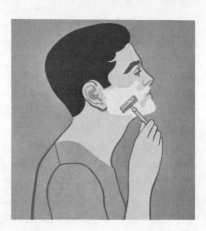

FIGURE 3

I might mention here what I will develop later on another aspect of the chemical reaction of sex. To illustrate. A mother says about her nine year old Johnny, "Oh, he's a real boy all right. He loves baseball, hates to eat vegetables, dislikes girls. . . ." These things are pretty true. Yet, as far as that last item goes, disliking girls, there's going to be a change. Johnny may still like baseball in the ninth grade and still hate vegetables but, suddenly, he no longer dislikes girls! What happened? Well, what did *not* happen was that Johnny sat down when he was fourteen and told himself that although he has refused to play with girls and couldn't stand those messy things ("No girls allowed" he wrote on top of his clubhouse when younger), it's about time he learned to live with them since they'll be around for a long time. No, Johnny has no such conversation with himself. Rather, what happens is that some of this chemical process of sex slowly begins to affect his brain and, little by little, from hating girls he learns to tolerate them and from toleration he learns to like them.

From the "girl-hater" of the fourth grade Johnny has emerged as the Junior Wolf of the eighth grade! Johnny's interest in girls and curiosity about sex in general—and yours—is the result of functioning sex glands, that's all. Johnny and you, from this point on, will begin to like many girls, then several girls, then a few girls, then one or two and then one day you'll be walking up the church aisle with your bride on your arm and God will be up in heaven chuckling, "Heh, Heh, faked you out, didn't I?" God has to fake you out. After all, if boys and girls who hate each other in the fourth grade grew up hating each other, no boy would ever ask a girl to marry him and soon the human race would end. So, it's fair enough of God to throw a little chemical magic around to get boys interested in girls.

Of all the wonderful operations of the boy's testicles, perhaps the manufacturing of the seed fluid is the most striking. As soon as his testicles begin causing all the other things we've mentioned, they also begin to manufacture a thickish white fluid containing millions of little *sperms* or *seeds*. These seeds can be seen only under a very powerful microscope. If you were to look at them through the microscope they would appear like little tadpoles or polywogs you used to catch in a lake or stream. As a matter of fact, there is a close resemblance. The sperm or seed is like a little tadpole in that it has a tail and it swims around in the seed fluid in quick motions. Now when a boy can produce this seed-containing fluid he can procreate. He can "create-for" God a living human being who will live on forever and ever. When a boy can produce this seed fluid he can become a father; he can have children. He can do by the gracious privilege of God something only God can do: he can create a creature with a body and soul and made to the image and likeness of God Himself!

Inside the sperms or seeds are little threads called chromosomes, and attached to these chromosomes, like buttons snapped on a string, are genes. This whole package, that is, the seed with its contents of chromosomes and genes, is the boy's contribution to the making of the baby. I don't want to go into too much science here since you get this in your science class, but heredity is a fascinating thing. For example, for every characteristic a boy has, he has a corresponding gene. His height, the color of his skin, the shape of his nose, the color of his eyes, etc. —each has a representative gene in the seed. Scientists have found out that certain genes are stronger than others and, when they meet, the stronger ones will "outvote" the weaker ones. For instance, (everything else being equal) if a brown-eyed person married a blue-eyed person the baby will have brown eyes since brown is a stronger gene or characteristic than blue. If a tall person marries a short person, the baby will be tall since the gene of tallness will outvote the gene for shortness. Scientists are now at a point where they can maneuver the genes and pretty soon parents will be able to put in an order for blond hair or blue eyes or even a boy or girl baby. Anyway, to get back to our point: when a boy can manufacture this whitish seed-containing fluid he is able to procreate; he now has the "stuff" with which he can produce a child.

There are two more matters we must discuss as we see how God has "tooled" the boy for his vocation in life. Normally the penis is in a soft and relaxed condition against the scrotum. Often, however, the penis can become enlarged and stiff and stand up straight. This hardening or stiffening of the penis is called an *erection*. Actually, boys have had erections before when young, but now it becomes more consciously pronounced, frequent and obvious. The medical explanation is that the penis is made up of sponge-like cells and you know what happens when a sponge is placed in water: it swells up. The same thing happens to the penis. When blood flows into the penis it swells up and stiffens and becomes erect. The boy has an erection.

Many things can cause the blood to flow into the penis and cause an erection, some which we call "sexy" and others not "sexy" at all. In the "sexy" category things like touching or playing with one's penis can produce the erection. Looking at a stimulating and sexy movie or reading a "dirty" book or just gazing at a well-built girl or meditating on some sexy scene in your imagination can all cause an erection. Of course, in this sense, boys are a little more fortunate than girls here because boys always know when they're getting excited or "shook up" about sex. That instant hard erection is a real reminder that they're getting hot and bothered, that they're sexually aroused. The caution signal is flashing! But non-sexy things can cause an erection also. Fright for one thing. Being nervous. Tension. Tight clothes. Many boys tell me they have erections when they go to bed and when they wake up in the morning. That's understandable. While they are up and around their blood is evenly distributed throughout the body. When they lay down the blood of the body, by the simple law of gravity, may shift to the center of the body, namely the sexual area, and cause the swelling of the penis.

One thing a boy has to get used to is that he cannot always control his erections. So many times they will happen automatically. They come and go even when he doesn't want them: in school, talking to a girl, in church! The average boy finds this embarrassing. Some boys have confided to me that they wear jock straps or athletic supporters to keep their erections down. Others resort to putting their hands in their pants pockets so that the shape caused by their hands will help camouflage the bulge caused by their erect penis. Ideally, since erections are perfectly normal and happen to every boy and will continue to happen until the day that he dies, a boy should not be embarrassed at all. However, in reality he is and he'll just have to sweat it out in public.

The Catholic boy wants to know if having an erection is a sin. We'll spell out the answers and its reasons in another chapter, but in general the answer is no. How could an erection be sinful? It's normal and natural. When it happens it happens. And when it happens it's enjoyable. Later we'll tell you that that nice feeling of erection is what we call a "primary sex pleasure" and it's a gift from God which He wants you to enjoy. The only time one might connect sin with an erection is when a boy might deliberately cause the erection on purpose merely to play with himself. The sin here, of course, could not be connected with sex since there is no sin connected with sex as God made it, but rather with the lack of respect for the sources of life. Any sin in this regard could only center around the lack of respect for what is sacred. But more of this in another chapter.

The other matter left to talk about is this: sometimes the testicles will produce an oversupply of the seed fluid.

When this occurs nature has a way of getting rid of it. What usually happens is that a boy is having a sexy dream (and again, since it is a dream, about sex, it's enjoyable—our primary sex pleasure again—and there is no sin here at all) and the dream becomes so intense that he suddenly wakes up and finds that the whitish seed fluid is pleasantly spurting out of his penis. The doctors call this occurrence a *"nocturnal emission"* or a *"wet dream."* This wet dream happens to every male and is perfectly normal. It's just nature's way of expelling the extra seed fluid. When this happens, wipe yourself off, and go back to sleep. If you're embarrassed about this perfectly natural (and holy) occurrence you'll have a tendency to hide your pajamas which by morning are dry but "starchy"; but if you're joyful about sex and really happy at these signs of your approaching manhood you won't hide them. Mom knows about these wet dreams and she too should rejoice at the growing up of her son. Something we'll speak of in this connection in another chapter is masturbation. This is deliberately causing the seed fluid to come out mostly by rubbing one's penis with the hand or rubbing it against the bed sheet, etc. Whether this is a sin or not we'll discuss in that chapter. The only caution here is that masturbation is habit-forming and, once started with any regularity, is awfully hard to stop. Masturbation is an enslaving habit that is most difficult to overcome.

To complete the picture of the male vocation, we should make mention of one further part of the male anatomy: the part the boy sits down on. Common street terms are "butt," "behind," "ass," "rear-end," etc. These terms are all right except that, like all such terms, they show a lack of education and a certain degree of uncomfortableness. Anyway, the correct term is *buttocks*. The buttocks are two large muscles and form a perfect padding for sitting comfort. The opening between the buttocks is called the anus or rectum. This is the opening from which solid waste matter (excretion or stool) is expelled. I would point out here that even the buttocks show forth the kindness of God. To illustrate, perform this simple experiment: stand up and feel your elbows. Now put your hands on your buttocks and press in and see if you can feel any bones there. You probably can't. Actually you have two pelvic points that are similar in sharpness to your elbow bones. Now if you sat down on those sharp pelvic bones without any cushioning you'd be in agony. It would be like sitting on a picket fence! So what did God do? He covered these two elbow-like bones with two large muscles so that you would be comfortable when you sat down. From parents' point of view the buttocks are ideal because they have enough nerve endings so that you felt it when you were spanked but the spanking couldn't damage you because there was so much padding there!

So, there we are: adolescence. Remember the meaning of the word? It means the "growing-up" time of a boy's life. It's the period of shuffling off the body and mind of a little boy and assuming the physical and mental structure of a man. The occurrence of this process, we must admit, is a nostalgic thing for a boy. After all, the little boy that you were was *so* comfortable. Outside of homework there wasn't much to worry about. Someone else did all the worrying (parents) and paid the bills and took care of you when you were sick and drove you to boy scouts and the ball games. You did have life pretty easy and it was *secure* being told what to wear, where to go and what time to go to bed even if you fussed a little about these things. But now? Now you're being forced out on your own. You're no longer merely an extension of your mother and father. You've got to sell yourself on your own terms. You've got to develop the kind of personality you want. You've got to be a person by yourself. And you have only a few years of adolescence in which to do this because, in a very short while, you'll be out of the house. You'll be off to college and finally married and you'll find yourself taking the responsibility of someone else. There's a struggle now to find out who and what you are and if you really can make it on your own. There are risks to growing up. But looked at in the right way another term for risk can be "adventure." It *is* an adventure to see yourself growing and watch your body growing and feeling your new sexual powers and drives. What you should do with these new and powerful emotions we'll discuss in another chapter, but they're there and they're yours and all the outward signs happening to you now, from that hair on your upper lip to your cracking voice, are signals that God is at work making you a man. To be a man is to have arrived. So the risks are worth it.

SUMMARY AND VOCABULARY

1. God invented two sexes because there are two major jobs to do in this world.
2. Sex refers to the specialized "tooling" of male and female that enables them to carry out their work.
3. In one sense, children are practically "sexless" or "untooled" because they have no responsibility and do not need as yet adult bodily and mental equipment.

4. Adolescence is the transition period whereby a child gets rid of the irresponsible infant body and assumes the mental and physical structures of adult life.

5. Adolescence is 'kicked off' by the pituitary "Alarm Clock" Gland which awakens the sex glands.

6. When awakened, these sex glands in turn produce their chemicals and pump them into the body to cause the internal and external changes to push a child into an adult.

7. One of the main functions of the sex glands is to produce "stuff" of procreation by which a person can now reproduce.

adolescence	—also called teen-age: the transition time from childhood to adulthood
testicles	—the male sex glands
scrotum	—the pouch suspended between the legs, that contains the testicles
penis	—the finger-like part of the male sexual organs
pubic hair	—the hair that grows around the sexual organs
seed-fluid	—the thickish, whitish fluid containing the sperms or seeds
seed or sperm	—the unit of procreation; the father's contribution to making of the baby; contains all the male characteristics
chromosomes	—the "thread" inside the seed to which are attached the genes
genes	—the unit of heredity; the unit of special characteristics
erection	—the stiffening of the penis caused by the in-flow of blood
nocturnal emission	—the wet dream: nature's way of expelling the stored up seed fluid
procreation	—literally, "to create on behalf of." To create on behalf of God; to produce a child

buttocks   —the two large muscles on which you sit
rectum or anus   —the opening between the buttocks from
                            which solid matter is expelled
urine   —the liquid waste matter expelled through
                            the penis
excretion   —sometimes called stool: solid waste matter
                            eliminated through the rectum

CHAPTER II

The Female Vocation

If the vocational engineering of the boy is marvelous, it is even more so for the girl. She is truly a wonderful design. Let us see why as we follow the progress of her development. Now she too has her "alarm clock" system and when her pituitary gland sends down the signal to her sex glands, she begins her slow process of leaving behind her little girl's body and assuming that of a mature woman. Adolescence begins her process of tooling for her vocation also. As you can see from Figure 4 her sex organs, unlike the boy's are inside her body. But her sexual organs have three parts also. Her sex glands are called *ovaries* (Latin for "egg-making"). These are equivalent to the male's testicles. Then there is the *womb* or *uterus*

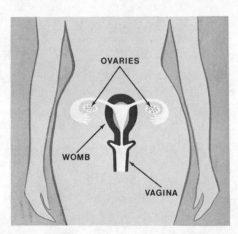

FIGURE 4

20

and finally the *vagina* or birth canal. Now when her ovaries are awakened by that chemical impulse from the pituitary gland they begin to manufacture their own chemicals and shoot them into the blood stream and all of the growing things happen to her: she grows taller, hair starts to grow between her legs, under arms, her hips become wider, her chest, which was as flat as yours, develops breasts, etc. In a word, she is chemically pushed into womanhood and prepared for possible motherhood.

Her ovaries or sex glands now produce the egg. Her egg is like the boy's seed in that it contains her chromosomes and genes and is *her* power of procreation. But unlike the boy who produces millions of seeds she produces only one mature egg and that only once a month. Let us take a look at this process.

When she starts to grow, which may be as early as the fourth and fifth grades, then once a month one ovary on one side of her body produces one egg which ripens. This ripened egg breaks out of the ovary and falls into a tube (the fallopian tube) and travels up and around towards the womb or uterus. As this journey is taking place, her womb, which is made up of spongy cells, is beginning to fill up with blood. This should lead you to guess that it has something to do with the baby. You would be right. The blood is getting stored up there to nourish the egg if it becomes ignited for a new life by the male seed (fertilized). However, if the egg is not to receive the male seed, then there is no need either for the egg or for the blood. Both simply wash away from the opening between her legs, the vagina (Figure 5 and 6). Then the next month the ovary on the other side produces a ripened egg; it travels down the fallopian tube to the womb. The womb fills up with blood and empties out if there is to be no baby. This cycle is repeated month after month with each ovary alternating in producing the egg. This whole complicated process is called *ovulation* (egg-producing) and menstruation (monthly blood-emptying). In menstruating the blood simply oozes out for a few days and that's that. Girls, when they start menstruating will wear some kind of sanitary napkin such as Tampex or Kotex which are simply compressed cotton to absorb the blood as it drains out. Unlike the boy who will produce seed until he dies, the girl will have this ovulation—menstruation cycle until she is about forty or forty-five and then she will stop. This stopping is called the change of life or *menopause* and when this happens a woman cannot have any more children because she is no longer producing eggs.

Since this is a book written for boys one or two considerations should be mentioned here. First, sometimes, menstruating for some girls can be upsetting, at least in

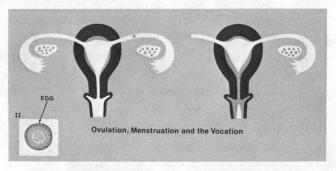

EGG

II

Ovulation, Menstruation and the Vocation

FIGURE 5   **FIGURE 6**

that sense that it might make them a little bit nauseous or uncomfortable. That's why you'll notice that sometimes during the month your sister or some girl in school you've been kidding around with or teasing doesn't respond or is peevish or irritable. She may be having her monthly period of menstruation. In three or four days she'll be back giving you a karate punch. So be a gentleman and try to understand. The other consideration is the change of life or menopause period. For some women this can be a very trying time of life. Well, you know how women are. They want to be young and beautiful always. But no matter how much makeup they use or whether they use Miss Clairol or not, they can't fool nature and when the change of life begins they might start feeling old and unattractive and become quite upset. This upsetment may last from months to years and men have to be understanding and patient. So, if your mother or aunt is in the forty to fifty bracket and you notice increasing irritability, crying for no reason at all—be kind. Perhaps they're going through the change of life and they'll need all the understanding and christian kindness they can get.

Now what happens when the egg is fertilized? Fertilization happens as a result of sexual intercourse. Sexual intercourse is difficult to talk about because it involves the deepest emotions known to man and is so very wrapped up with love. At your age you haven't grown into deep kind of love yet. It's not your fault. Love has to be learned and it has to grow and be refined with experience. Your lack of experience in love makes it hard to get across the act and meaning of sexual intercourse. But I will try at least on the basis of what you know.

Let us begin by pointing out that a synonym for sexual

intercourse is often the phrase "sexual love." This phrase carries a little more meaning but both terms are acceptable. Now love has but one object and that is union, togetherness. You verify this all the time. You have a buddy. Every time we see him, we see you. At recess time you're together, after school, maybe you even play on the same ball team. If you like someone you want to be with them, close to them. This instinct to be with the one you love is both natural and desirable. You have and have had other experiences of wanting to be close to the one or thing you love even though you may be too old to remember now. If you have very small brothers and sisters you can see this on them. I bet that when *you* were a baby you had some old toy, say, a horsie or teddy bear that you brought to bed with you. Your mother couldn't even get the dirty old thing away from you to wash it because you screamed your head off. And you took your teddy bear or whatever it was and squeezed it and almost hugged the stuffing out of it. You may reply that this was kind of childish and foolish; but I answer that it wasn't. Once more, God built it into man that if he loves something very, very much he wants to be one with it and your hugging the teddy bear was simply a proof of this. When you were five or six years old you threw your arms around Mommy and nearly choked her to death. You don't do this so much now that you're grown up. You probably think it's sissy. Anyway, it's just as well you don't; with your new body and new strength and muscles you'd probably give your mother a half nelson and cripple her! But your instinct was true. The hugging was the outward sign of your inner desire to be together with her in happiness.

We see this same principle at work in Jesus' love for us. He wanted so literally to be one with us that He invented a sacrament of unity, Holy Communion. Communion means "union with." Jesus wanted this union with us so badly that He found a way that we could "eat Him up." You've heard women using the same expression when they were cooing over a cute baby. They exclaimed, "Oh, he's so precious. I could just eat him up!" Even they were saying what God put into their hearts: that if they desire and love something or someone they want to be together with it. "Eating a person up" is the closest you can come in creating togetherness!

But not quite. God invented an even closer union of love. He expressed it, as the Bible relays His words, that a couple who truly love each other could become "two in one flesh." Jesus repeated the Father's words by reminding us that "they are no longer two, but one flesh." That's a pretty close union, two separate people blending as one. But that's precisely what happens in sexual intercourse. Let's backtrack a little. There came a time when a boy and a girl asked each other to do something very difficult and only a strong love would enable them to do it. They asked each other to leave their very own homes, their mothers and fathers, brothers and sisters, bedroom and family belongings and come and live with each other and start a new family unit. So they did, but only because, once more, their love for each other was stronger than their love for their own homes and their own comfort. So these two got married and wanted to express their togetherness and really to become the one unit they were now supposed to be as husband and wife. These two wanted to obey God and become one flesh and they would do this in the wonderful way that God provided. They would partake of the holy communion of sexual intercourse. At night the husband would tell his wife of his love for her, kiss her tenderly and then lay gently on top of her. At the moment of greatest warmth he will insert his erect penis into her vagina and in that "two-in-one flesh" embrace they will be truly as one and love will be satisfied. This man and woman were now doing in great depth and beauty what they did on a less important level from the time they hugged their teddy bears to the time they put their arm around a friend.

Besides being the great outward sign, the great sacrament of their love, sexual intercourse would provide another most intimate opportunity. At the end of this sexual union the seed fluid of the husband would be ejected into his wife's vagina. This is how the seed passes over from father to mother. Now millions of his tail-propelled seed go in search of an egg (Figure 7). If there is no egg the

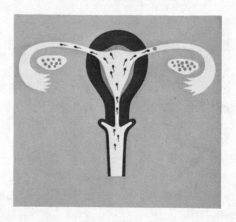

FIGURE 7

seed will eventually die and no child will be conceived. But if there is an egg in the fallopian tube or the womb at the time then one of the seeds can finally find it and penetrate it. All the other seeds or sperms simply die. It's a question of the first seed to reach the egg, wins. In any case fertilization has taken place—the father's seed has entered the mother's egg—and the miracle of life is about to begin. That this miracle has started is first known to the wife when she doesn't have her monthly period at the next regular time. If her blood is not washing away, then it's staying inside her womb and if it's staying inside then it's only for one reason: she's going to have a baby! She announces to her husband that she is pregnant and a visit to the doctor verifies this.

Now the continuing miracle is that this egg begins to split. Then it resplits and multiplies into four, then eight, sixteen, thirty two and so on. By some mystery which the doctors still have not unravelled, the cell is programmed to split into various types; certain cells go into skin cells, some into tissue, some into bone, enamel, hair, etc. (Fig-

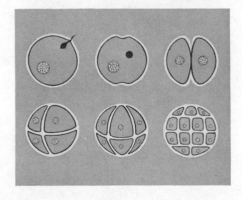

FIGURE 8

ure 8). Meanwhile, during all this multiplication of the cells the elastic womb is stretching to accommodate them. As you know it takes nine months for all the cells to be developed into a fully formed baby.

Inside the mother's womb the baby is situated as illustrated in Figure 9. Notice several clever (clever of God, that is) things. The baby is upside down. This makes it easier for him to come out of the womb and also keeps the blood, by gravity, going to the brain. He is encased in a sac of birth fluid which has the same purpose as the fluid in a door jam: it absorbs any shock. The baby gets his food and oxygen through a tube (the umbilical cord) from the wall of the mother's womb into his stomach. So there he is, snug as a bug in a rug. He's getting free food, free air, free warmth and free transportation. After nine months it's time for the baby to stop freeloading on Mom and to be born. The mother goes to the hospital where the doctor can help her since he has examined her and knows the exact position of the baby. The upper muscles

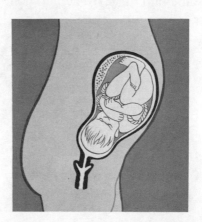

FIGURE 9

of the mother's womb begin to contract and start to force the baby out of the vagina or birth canal. These contractions of the womb muscles are called labor pains. Finally, like the mouth of a balloon the vagina stretches wide, the baby passes through and is born. The cord is cut and the little remaining cord on the baby's stomach will eventually form into a kind of scab and fall off. This scar you call your "belly-button" but which the doctors call a navel. All the other organs of the mother's body which were pushed aside to make room for the baby growing large in her womb, fall back into place and in a short time she is her old self and old shape again.

Meanwhile, while the mother was carrying the child in her womb her breasts were getting larger and filling up with a special formula baby milk. When the baby is born the mother feeds him at her breast as he draws this milk from them. Here, perhaps, is the best time to make some comments on the female breasts. A woman has breasts for two rather important reasons. One is, as we have indicated, to feed her child her milk. The other, however, is also quite important. Doctors and psychologists say that a mother must hold the baby close to her breasts and cuddle him and let him know that he is wanted and loved (Figure 10). They say that if the baby is not wanted or loved, if the baby is rejected and not cuddled against the mother then the baby may die or if he grows up, may be a mental patient. Mother's acceptance and love are more important, apparently, than food. It is at mother's breasts that his love is first had. Even small children lay their heads on mother's breasts and tell her their sorrows and troubles and receive there their warmth and reassurance.

Unfortunately, in our society a woman's breasts are

FIGURE 10

supposed to be "sexy" in the stupidest sense of the word. A girl may try to emphasize them or wear her dress just low enough so that she's playing peek-a-boo with her breasts. In other cultures women don't even wear anything over their breasts and maybe that's a saner approach. It's too bad you don't witness your mother or someone else's mother feeding her baby at her breasts. It's a beautiful sight and will give a boy a good common sense knowledge of what the female breasts are really for.

So, it takes three to create a baby. The father who donates the seed, the mother who donates the egg and God who donates the soul. To Catholic boys a lot of this should not really be new. They've been hearing about such things for years even though they never realized it. For example, around Christmas time you hear read the Gospel of St. Luke which has an awful lot to do with sex. It goes like this:[1]

> Now in the sixth month the angel Gabriel was sent from
> God to a town of Galilee called Nazareth, to a virgin be-
> trothed to a man named Joseph . . . and when the angel
> had come to her he said, "Hail, full of grace, the Lord is
> with thee . . ." And the angel said to her, "Do not be
> afraid, Mary, for thou hast found grace with God. Be-
> hold thou shall conceive in thy womb and shall bring
> forth a son; and thou shall call his name Jesus . . ." But
> Mary said to the angel, "How shall this happen since I
> do not know man?" And the angel answered and said to
> her, "The Holy Spirit shall come upon thee and the
> power of the most high shall overshadow thee; and
> therefore the Holy One to be born shall be called the
> Son of God . . ." Mary said, "Behold the handmaid of
> the Lord; be it done to me according to thy word."
> (Luke 1:26ff)

Now notice several things here. First of all, the angel
used "sex" terms like "conceive" and "womb." Mary was
pure and one of the reasons she was was that she really
understood sex. She didn't get upset at the angel's greet-
ing, grab a broom and start chasing him around the room
crying, "Get out of here, you dirty angel!" No, she took
the message and understood its sexual implications very
well: she was going to have a baby grow inside her
womb. But she had a very sensible question—and it is interesting to know that Mary's first recorded words are a
sex question! She said, "How shall this happen since I do
not know man?" That word "know" in Hebrew is not like
our "know" in the sense of understanding or recognition.
"To know" in the Bible means sexual intercourse.
("Adam knew Eve and she bore a son.") That's why the
Oxford Bible (Protestant) translates Mary's question as,
"How can this be when I have no husband" and the Jeru-

salem Bible says, "How can this be since I am a virgin?"
Mary, then, is simply asking a question about sex. She is
saying in so many words, "Yes, all right, I am going to
have a baby. But how can I have a child when I haven't
made sexual love, haven't had intercourse?" And the
angel is replying, "Well, that's a good question. But in
your case the egg inside of your womb is going to grow
without any seed from Joseph or any man. The Holy
Spirit will come upon you and work this miracle." If
you're real sharp you'll notice that the Church has ar-
ranged this message of the angel as the Feast of the An-
nunciation, March 25th—just nine months to December
25th, the birth of Our Lord!

We ourselves repeat some of the sex words even when
we pray. We say, ". . . blessed are thou among women
and blessed is the fruit of thy *womb,* Jesus. . . ." Yes,
Jesus is the result or product or fruit of Mary's womb just
as we are the fruits of our mothers' wombs. You see the
holiness connected with sex! How unfortunate man introduced shame and sin, smeared out the word JOY that
God had written about sex and wrote instead the word
EVIL.

So, there we are: the anatomy of sexual vocations.
Two beings to run the world, two sexes working together
to make this a better planet. Man and woman are partners in this mutual effort. They do not, of course, have to
be married. Even the single man or woman still help each
other and have his and her own special outlook and brand
of help to offer to the world. But married as husband and
wife or unmarried as celibates man and woman are equal
partners in the creation of a better world.

SUMMARY AND VOCABULARY

1. Adolescence for the female "tools" her for her vocation in life.
2. Her sexual organs are internal, consisting of the ovaries, the womb and the vagina.
3. Each month a female ovulates and menstruates: that is, she produces an egg, the womb fills up with blood and both discharge from the vagina if there is to be no baby. This whole process is called ovulation and menstruation.
4. This process continues until middle age when it stops (menopause).
5. If she is to have a child, she needs the seed from a male. This seed is transferred during sexual intercourse.
6. Sexual intercourse is a profound and God-invented means of the deep closeness of love between a man and a woman.
7. When the man's seed penetrates the woman's egg, fertilization occurs.
8. The egg multiplies in the ever stretching womb until the baby is formed after a nine month period.
9. After nine months, the baby is born through the vagina or birth canal.
10. The baby is fed and loved at the mother's breasts.

ovaries	—the two female sex glands producing the eggs
womb	—also called uterus. The place where the baby grows
vagina	—the entrance to the womb and passageway for the baby
menstruation	—also called the "monthly period"; the monthly flow of blood discharged from the womb when no baby is to be born
ovulation	—the releasing of the egg from the ovary

egg	—also called "ova"; the unit of heredity containing the female chromosomes and genes
umbilical cord	—the tube through which oxygen and food go to the baby and waste matter passes from the baby
navel	—also called belly button; the remaining 'scar' where the umbilical cord used to be
placenta	—sometimes called "the afterbirth"

CHAPTER III

Sexual Joy

Joy. Have you ever stopped to think just how much sheer joy there is having a human body? In fact, there are so many joys attached to the body that we take them for granted. In this chapter we're going to dwell on a basic truth about these bodily joys; namely, that they are all *purposeful* joys. The joys of the human body are for a purpose; they are always bestowed for the benefit of the person and of the human race.

Take eating. If food tasted so awful, like eating ashes or stones, no one would eat. Perhaps the doctors would have to render us unconscious and get the food into our veins while we were "out of it." But if no one ate, we would soon become weakened, subject to disease and die. Even now, on a small scale people will neglect eating. In your old movies the mad scientist is so busy down his cellar making monsters that he doesn't even take time out to eat. You do the same thing in your own way. Your mother says, "For the last time, turn off that television set and come and eat!" You realize, of course, that the human race itself is at stake if no one eats. So God provided. He made food *taste good* and that usually is a pretty good inducement for us to eat. The joys and pleasures of eating are God's "come-on" to take on the responsibility of keeping healthy bodies. The taste pleasure of food, in other words, has a purpose.

Or take sleeping. Without sleep our bodies would not

35

have time to repair themselves and, if this went on for a long enough time, we would die. That's why one of the chief forms of torture is to keep a prisoner awake. God's device to entice us to sleep is pleasure. Pleasure with a purpose. Think how good you feel when, after a hard day playing football, you stretch out at night in bed, snuggle under the covers and fall off to sleep. Take going to the bathroom. There's joy, the joy of relief, in eliminating the waste matter in going to the bathroom. Your body takes food or fuel into itself, draws out the nourishment and leaves the "ashes" or waste—just like a campfire or furnace. To get rid of the "ash" or waste matter feels good. You might give an audible sigh of relief when you've gone to the bathroom. That's the body's way of expressing the joy of eliminating waste matter that, if left in the body, would poison it. Once more, joy with a purpose.

The joys of the body, then, are shrewdly related to the body's health and lead people to take on the responsibilities of keeping well. So it is with sex. Most of all with sex. There is a joy and excitement to it, the *sexual pleasure* we call it. And this joy is one of our strongest because the job it's meant to fulfill is one of the hardest. The sexual joy has a purpose. Let's examine this purpose.

We'll approach it this way. In your mind at least, take a piece of paper, draw a line down the center, and on one side list some of the freedoms you will have to surrender when you get married and some of the obligations you will have to assume. Such a list might include such items of surrender as:

Money. Before you're married, who can you spend all of your money on? Right, yourself! If you're a young man in the working field you can save your money and get yourself a new Mustang or GTO, buy the best liquor and have the sharpest clothes. If you want to be deceitful you can even call up your boss and tell him you're sick and just sack out in bed all day. What's one day's pay to a free and easy bachelor? But when married? Well, that's going to be a different story. The mortage is due, there are doctor's bills on your desk, the kids need clothes to begin school, the payments on the car are behind and so on. I'm sure you've seen this with your own parents. They do without in order to take care of the family properly. When's the last time they had a vacation—that is, away from you and the others, just by themselves? How old is Dad's suit and overcoat? I know one man who told me that he had to give up even his beer and cigarette money because he has six kids and he has to buy them shoes for the start of school. And, about calling the boss and telling him you're sick: well, even if Dad *is* feeling kind of sick he'll go to work. He can't afford to lose a day's pay.

Going out. Before you're married you can go out every night if you want to. And you can go wherever you want and with whom you want and you can keep all the late hours you want. Once you're married you'll have to stay home. For one thing, as we indicated above, you won't be able to afford going out every night. But another thing is that you have cares at home. Maybe the wife is sick or one of the children. You'll have to help with the homework (even the new math!), repair the house, dole out the discipline and balance the budget.

Other women. Before you're married you can play the field. You can be the town's Greatest Lover. A brunette one night, a redhead another and a blond another. You can be God's gift to womanhood! Once you're married

—well, any wife is going to take a rather dim view of such extracurricular activities. No, once you're married, it's one woman and one woman only until "death do you part." You'll have to bypass (except for an admiring glance) all of the other gorgeous and shapely girls in the world—millions of them!—and stay true to one. The pursuit of other females ends with marriage.

Family life. Before marriage you have only yourself really to worry about. No baby disturbing a night's sleep for the bachelor, no snoring wife and no flushing toilets in the middle of the night. Just yourself. Peaceful. But after marriage there's much concern and much taking care of others. Your son is sick and you're up with him at four o'clock. If you can get back to sleep at five you still have to get up at six to go to work. Your daughter is having her tonsils out and you have to run to the hospital after work. Your wife calls you on the phone. Johnny's just smashed his finger in the door jam and she's calling from the emergency ward. Your kids will come home to your house, eat food that you've bought, watch a TV set that you purchased and sleep in a bed that you've provided. You or your wife will clean up after your child vomits all over the floor. You or your wife (with wrinkled noses) many times will wipe off the dirty behind of your infant son or daughter.

Well, you get the point. There's a lot of freedoms to surrender when you get married and a lot of responsibility to take on. Do you think that any sensible and sane person, weighing the two, would ever get married? I don't think so. Or at least they would hesitate an awful lot. And if no one got married that would soon end the human race, and God certainly did not want this to happen. So He provided. He did for sex exactly what He did for food and sleep and every other necessary and human function: He attached pleasure with a purpose. He made sex enjoyable and pleasurable to get people to use it so they would take on the responsibilities we've just mentioned above. If the eating pleasure is attached to the responsibility of nutrition and the sleeping pleasure is attached to the responsibility of repairing the body, the sex pleasure is attached to the responsibility of marriage, providing and taking care of others.

Of course it is obvious that people can frustrate God's design. People can become so attached to the eating pleasure that they practically neglect the nutritional aspect and just eat for the sake of eating. Doing this to excess is called gluttony. Over-claiming the sleeping pleasure is called sloth. Over-indulging the drinking pleasure is called drunkenness. These pleasures are attached to purposes, responsibilities; they cannot exist merely for their own sake.

Sexual pleasure is attached very much to responsibility and, although in the next chapter we'll talk about sex and morality, we can give a quick statement about the use of the sex pleasure here: the deliberate pleasures of sex are "purpose pleasures"; they are attached to the responsibilities of marriage. They don't exist for their own sake and therefore any deliberate use of sex outside of marriage responsibility is wrong. This statement is not so world-shaking however. It's pretty much the same rule you use for everything else in life. If you studied and the teacher gave your buddy the hundred you'd be mad. Especially if he never studies. Your argument would be based exactly on the principal involved in sexual morality: if you did the

work, you deserve the mark. And you're right. If your
buddy worked all week and his boss gave you his pay,
he'd be mad. For you to receive the pay without taking
on the responsibility is unfair. Correct. That's all we're
saying about the pleasures of sex. If you're ready for the
hardship and surrenders of family life, you may have the
reward of the sexual pleasures; if not, no. To steal the deliberate use and pleasures of sex without its responsibilities is no different than stealing the mark without the
studying or stealing the pay without the work. Rewards
and pleasures have a purpose and you've got to take the
whole package. Bodily joys are purposeful. Good sense
and christian morality (the same thing) tell us not to separate them.

But we must hit the balance here. We've got to be careful that ugly suspicion doesn't creep in and destroy the
whole concept of joy. Sexual suspicion is an awful thing
and can lead to the extreme of thinking that *anything* to
do with sexual pleasure before marriage is wrong. So to
put this suspicion to rest let us make a very careful distinction between the two kinds of sexual pleasure. Sexual
pleasure is divided into the *primary* and the *secondary*
joys of sex. Let's see what they are and who's entitled to
either or both.

The *primary* joys of sex are those we've already mentioned; They are the joys connected with just being a boy.
A boy feels happy with his body, he is comfortable with
it, he enjoys it. He likes to eat, he likes to sleep, he likes
to go to the bathroom. The adolescent boy has even more
to rejoice about. He knows what's happening to him as he
grows towards manhood. He's read books such as this
one and has freed himself from any shame connected

with his body. He enjoys having sexual organs, he is very pleased with the pubic hair growing around them, he gives a happily embarrassed smile when his voice cracks in front of company. He is pleased every time he has an erection and he is doubly thrilled if, when he's sleeping, he has a really sexy dream that causes him to wake up feeling the pleasant sensation of the seed fluid oozing out of his penis. He marvels at how quickly he's aroused, how many erections he gets every time he meets a certain girl. He can stand naked in front of a mirror and be pleased with his body. He can glance out of the corner of his eye in the shower room at another boy's sexual organs and happily compare them to his own. He likes flexing his newly formed muscles. He enjoys the feel of his legs and thighs and buttocks. He is happy with his body that can dance so wildly to loud music and lean into the wind as he zooms down the street on his Honda. He likes to soak up the sun at the shore and he likes the taste of a hot pizza. He rejoices that he can maneuver his body in sports and bend it low in worship. If he were familiar with Scripture and if he were inclined to do so, he would stand up in the middle of history class and shout with King David, "I give you thanks that I am so wonderfully made. Wonderful are your works!" (Ps. 138) A boy is pleased with his body and its reactions. He *is* his body. Such, then, are the primary pleasures of sex: the normal, spontaneous, free-flowing feelings of bodily reactions and sensations. The primary pleasures of sex are all those indeliberate "alivenesses" of the human body. Every boy at any age, especially the adolescent boy, is entitled to these.

Beyond these built-in, spontaneous primary joys of sex there are what we call the *secondary* joys. What are these joys? These are the deliberate sexual-organ joys *done on purpose*. These are the deliberate, planned and purposeful joys of sexual-organ arousement. These are the more exact joys that God put into sex's immediate use in order to get people to take on the responsibilities of married life that ordinarily they might not want to. These are the joys belonging to married people, that is, people who have freely stood before the Church and before the State and openly and publicly declared their willingness to take on the responsibilities of family life, children, hospitalization, the monthly mortgage, sickness and general worryment that goes into the raising of a family. These secondary joys are the joys that husband and wife deliberately accept as a gift from God since they have pledged the responsibilities that go with them. The secondary joys of sex are the deliberate sexual arousements of the human body.

A few examples will make the distinction between the primary and secondary joys apparent. In an actual case I'll cite later, a boy is changing classes. For some reason the corridor of the school is unusually crowded and there's much shoving and pushing. Accidentally one of the most gorgeous and luscious females in the school gets pushed flat against him. He smells her perfume and feels her stomach and breasts crush against him. As a normal boy he becomes aroused and his penis hardens instantly. He should say two things to the girl. He should say, "Excuse me" and she'll understand that. If he's sexually sophisticated he should also say, "Thank you" and maybe she won't understand that. Actually he's thanking her for an unexpected bodily sexual pleasure of an erection. He's thanking her for the indeliberate *primary* joy of sex that she brought his way and made an otherwise boring school day quite memorable. Contrast this with the boy who, parked with a girl, "makes out," touches her breasts and generally "pets" her. Naturally he's getting very aroused; in fact, he has just as hard an erection as the boy in the corridor. What's the difference? The difference is that in the school situation, there was a case of the indeliberate primary joys and in the car there is a case of the deliberate and purposeful secondary joys. But to steal in a premeditated way these joys and deliberately separate them from all responsibilities is immoral. The couple in the car have not pledged children, sickness, bills, hardship. They're not different at all from our example of the boy who wants the good mark without the studying or the pay check without the work. There is sin in the second case. No sin connected with sex, of course; but sin for taking something so meaningful and beautiful as sex and using it for pleasure only outside the confines of responsibility. Its "sexual drunkedness"—going out of one's way for the pleasure and not caring for the purpose for which the pleasure was put there in the first place.

Another example. A husband is making love to his wife. He touches her and they tenderly caress each other. They become aroused. His penis hardens, becomes erect and he inserts it into his wife's vagina in the warm, exciting and joyous act of sexual intercourse. This is, as we've indicated in the previous chapter, a wonderful and beautiful moment, a holy one as the two of them become "one flesh." They are partaking of the sacrament of Matrimony just as if they were both kneeling at the altar rail together receiving Holy Communion. In fact, this intercourse *is* their holy communion. Moreover, their sexual act is not only filled with intense joy (secondary joys) but is precisely an outward sign of taking responsibility for each other not only for now but for tomorrow and forever: in sickness and in health, for richer and for poorer, for better or for worse until death parts them. Contrast this with the boy and girl sneaking off to a motel and having sexual intercourse. The act indeed is the same but there is terrible sin here. Again, not because sex is evil, but because they took that which said "responsibility" and did not accept responsibility. They don't *want* the responsibility in fact; they only want the secondary sex pleasure without its purpose. They're stealing the secondary pleasures of sex and isolating it from the total responsibility of living and working and praying and dying together. For this boy and girl, the intercourse was a selfish act of deliberately using the secondary pleasures of sex without purpose. Being selfish, it is sinful.

A final example. A boy, with deliberate premeditation arouses himself. He takes all the deliberate sexual-organ pleasures of sex. His deliberate erection, his deliberate sensations, his deliberate ejection of his seed fluid—all are meant for responsible relationship with another. What the boy has done is to take the joys, not shared them with another in responsibility, but turned them back on himself. As a solitary, selfish act it is sinful. It is pleasure without purpose.

I hope these examples make clear the difference between the primary and secondary pleasures of sex. The main difference, as you can see, is in the *deliberateness*. But the primary joys of sex are wider than just a question of deliberateness. Once more, they are all those attitudes of being pleased with having a body, all those activities and sensations that come from the use of the body whether it's taking a warm shower or running down the ball field for a touchdown. The primary joys of sex include all the indeliberate sexual-organ reactions and delights from a spontaneous erection to the accidental "feel" of a girl. The secondary joys of sex on the other hand are those that are sought after primarily in the sexual area; they are all those joys connected specifically with the sexual organs and deliberately brought on by the person himself. Such deliberate sexual-organ joys belong to the married. They exist as the "thank you" from God to parents who have pledged themselves to the responsibilities of family life. They are the joys with a purpose.

Let us now apply these distinctions to questions of thoughts. The subject of sexual thoughts or "dirty" thoughts is a very difficult one to handle. The average adolescent boy with his rich imagination has a great deal of trouble with "dirty" thoughts and is never sure that he's safe from sin. Moreover, the Catholic boy has been warned, either directly or indirectly, of the danger of a moral chain reaction. Once he gives in to a sexual thought or fantasy or some flitting picture in his mind, then this will immediately cause daydreaming, sexual arousal and finally some sexual activity such as petting or masturbation. The best tactic therefore, he is cautioned, is to "resist the beginnings" and he'll have no problem with bad results.

The problem with such advice is that it says too much. It demands almost the impossible. Every human being has an imagination life which can be repressed but not stopped. Fantasies, images, mental pictures flit in and out of one's head almost constantly. Who is the boy who hasn't pictured himself as the big-league hero, the "big man on campus," the world's greatest lover? Even Snoopy indulges his fantasies in his encounters with the "Red Baron"! The mind or imagination is like a never turned off TV screen and everything flashes on the screen. In short, fantasies are normal. They're a part of every person's life and even quite important in maintaining good balance. For example, fantasies about being a better student with its rewards, becoming a great basketball player with its fame, etc., can provide good motivation to reach these goals. Cornelia Otis Skinner in her book *Madame Sarah* tells us that at nine years old Sarah Bernhardt had visions of herself as the world's greatest actress—which one day she did become. Fantasies can test what is real as when a person imagines a future event and plans how he'll handle it. Fantasy can be a kind of rehearsal for the real thing. Fantasy or imaginations can also be a pretty good buffer between unpleasant reality and almost complete frustration. Reliving an argument with your father, for example, thinking of all the things you should have and could have said to him, can blow off steam. Going over in your mind what you might have said to the girl you like so much can pass off some of the tensions of a clumsy encounter with her earlier in the day.

What I am trying to say, then, is that not all imaginations of the mind, all fantasies are bad or useless or harmful. Like anything else in life, of course, fantasies can become harmful when excessive. Through excessive fantasy a person can slip out of reality altogether. The fantasy that one is Napoleon will only lead him to the nut house. This is a fantasy that went too far and lost contact with reality. As with all things the amount of fantasy in a person's life varies from person to person. Some kids have real wild imaginations, some very pale and inactive ones. However, although the power of imagination and daydreaming may vary from person to person, it is consistent within the same person.

Each boy has to determine the extent of his own fantasy life; how powerful his imagination is, how likely or not to pull him too far; how well defined the line between imagining something and actually doing it. A boy might picture himself as the gunman Clyde with Bonnie, his moll, at his side but he knows that doesn't mean that he's going to run out and shoot people. Only a person whose fantasy became very excessive and overpowering would do such a thing. No, the average boy will picture himself as the gunman, enjoy his brief movie scene of mowing down the cops, but he will not kid himself that all this is real or spend all day at it. Most boys soon learn to determine the extent of their fantasy tolerance.

Fantasies, naturally, include those of sex. Imaginations of nude girls, sexual intercourse and such are bound to flit on the TV set of every adolescent boy's imagination. These fantasies, like all the others, will be as strong or weak depending on each boy's temperament. Some will arouse a boy to action (v.g. masturbation); some will be merely a pleasant source of enjoyment flashing on the mind and not lead to any deed whatever. All incidents of sexual fantasy, however, are likely to be termed as "dirty" thoughts and sins. But this is not necessarily so at all.

As we pointed out above, some boys will so linger and become so preoccupied that they're the gunman, Clyde, that they'll go out and shoot someone. Other boys will enjoy the momentary identity with Clyde and go about their business. So, too, with sexual thoughts and imaginations. Not all of them will necessarily lead to impure actions. Since not all of them will, it remains for each boy to learn his own tolerance and where he must draw the line. In fact, a boy's first step in coming to terms with sexual thoughts is *self-acceptance*. He accepts the fact that sexual impulses are a normal part of his life. He accepts them with the same matter-of-fact realization that he accepts that food appetite impulses are a part of his life, especially if he's hungry. He accepts himself as normally well adjusted knowing full well that there's a big difference between his fantasies and his actions and he is not worried that he can't control the situation. As a result of his self-acceptance he's not frightened. In fact, he rather enjoys himself. After all, he *is* a sexual being, he *is* responsive to sexual stimulation, he has experienced the primary pleasures of sex. With such a powerful force in his life it would indeed be unusual that sex would not often and pleasantly invade his fantasy life.

So, to the question of sin. Are these sex fantasies sinful? Are "dirty" thoughts sinful? The answer obviously is, "It all depends." It all depends on the distinction between normal, passing sex imaginations (primary pleasure) and the preoccupation with them (secondary pleasure). Sexual fantasies such as a boy's mental image of an attractive nude girl is almost involuntary and quite common. Short daydreams about the sexual activities of either sex are also quite normal. Most boys, most people, have these spontaneous sexual fantasies daily. As free, spontaneous sex fantasies they fall into the category of primary sex pleasures and are completely allowable. They are normal

and sinless and remain so as long as a boy is not constantly seeking such thoughts, constantly and deliberately
drooling over sexy magazines to induce fantasy, constantly and deliberately encouraging such things to the
point of arousal. If he does this then he's in the realm of
the secondary sex pleasures to which he has no right. In
other words, *when sexual imaginations, thoughts, passing
mental images and fantasies stop being a diversion and
become a preoccupation, they are sinful.* Again, we're
really talking about the primary and secondary pleasures
of sex. In short, there's all the difference in the world between the fleeting fantasy provoked by a pretty girl in a
bikini (primary sex pleasure) and a lengthy, deliberate
and well-lingered daydream in response to a sexy picture
in a magazine (secondary sex pleasure).

"What about me?" you might say. Well, what's your
tolerance? You can and should enjoy the primary pleasures of the spontaneous, unprovoked sexual images in
your mind. You should be able in passing to enjoy the
sexual fantasy of a pretty girl in a tight sweater or the
sight of a sexy calendar. You should be able without sin
to brush your eyes over a group of paperbacks or glance
at your naked buddies in the dressing room. You know
how far you can go. There is, of course, some risk and
you should not over-tease yourself, but in general the risk
is preferable to going to the other extreme. This extreme
would be to immediately and automatically censor out
any beginnings of any sexual thoughts or feelings. This
extreme would be an immediate and anxious reaction
against any sexual fantasy that just floated by in the
mind's eye. Since sexual fantasies are frequent and daily
for the average adolescent boy, he's going to get awfully

tired trying to keep vigilance over every such fantasy. He'll probably get guilt-ridden or scrupulous or he'll so try to suppress such things that they'll pop out anyway to cause him further anxiety. Sexual fantasies are a part of life and a legitimate source of the primary sexual joys. To confess every such passing fantasy or imagination as "dirty" thoughts is to be unreal and to reject the primary pleasures of sex that God wants you to have. Sin enters, as we've said before, at the point of emotional preoccupation, at the point of deliberateness, at the fully-realized delay of the secondary sex pleasures.

In closing it might be helpful to extend our remarks and apply them to the common experiences of books, movies and magazines. Perhaps the quickest thumbnail rule for spotting the truly trashy and impure book, movie or magazine is our clue to impure thoughts: *preoccupation*. There's no "context." Everything points to sex or the sex act without any redeeming context of interpretation or respect or genuine human concern. The point is just kicks. No human value, just kicks. Just an absorption with sex for its own sake. There's no proportion to anything else. The book, movie or magazine merely exists to cause sexual arousal to the onlooker, period.

Books. Our rule of preoccupation can be easily applied to most books although there will always be borderline cases. You can have, for example, a case of adultery in the classic by Sigrid Undset in *Kristin Lavransdatter* where the sexual values are ultimately woven into human life values. Or you can have the eventually tiresome sexual mating in every other paragraph of some of our modern novels. In this latter case sex *is* preoccupying and definitely not a part of the larger context of human values.

Catcher in the Rye can take you to an adolescent's world
where a boy takes off a girl's bra or sees "fuck" written
on apartment house walls, but the book poses ultimate
value questions and sex is in context, an interest and a
challenge and not a preoccupation overruling every other
consideration of human life.

Movies can be highly significant contributions to
seeing and catching human nature and trying to put sex
into context. Or they too can be trashy and have as their
only motivation unhealthy preoccupation. Movies like
Alfie and *Georgie Girl* and *Rachel, Rachel* can be fairly
explicit about sex and nudity, but place such things in the
genuine context of human experience. The ramifications
and effects on human beings is clearly shown. Sex in
these and like pictures is "contextual," an interest and a
commentary—not a preoccupation. Usually the most ar-
tistically done movies are the most moral. Other movies
with such juvenile titles like *Franny's Fat Fanny* or *Hot
Night of Lust* and the like with their advertisements
promising "unnatural lust" or "shocking sex," etc. can be
nothing but reel after reel of inane sexual activity, eventually boring, that says nothing and is its own excuse.
The new movie ratings of "G" for General audiences,
"M" for Mature audiences (guided here by parents), "R"
for Restricted movies to persons over 16 unless accompanied by an adult and "X" restricted only to persons over
16 are most helpful. This system takes into account that
adults are more discriminating and can bring both context and humor to movies explicit about sex. Adolescents,
with their newly found passions, can seldom do either:
they have not experience and their humor about sex is
too serious and symptomatic. In the "M" and "R" movies

you will react to their sexual stimulation but such movies, if they are truly artistic, will have a sensible and telling context and as such will present a passing impact and not a sin.

Magazines. Some magazines are truly "contextual." Some present nudity with dignity and humanity. Other magazines are the girlie magazines showing half naked girls in all kinds of provocative poses. Their purpose is out and out stimulation. There is absolutely no context whatsoever. This is perversion for its own sake. The tendency is to make the male viewer see woman solely in terms of breasts and buttocks. A woman, *any* woman—is surely more than that. Every woman is a *person*. The trouble with the girlie magazines is that they are antifeminine; they lower the emotional and mental image of womanhood and as such are printed lies.

So, we're back to joy again. God is Joy itself and wishes us to share it. Bodily joys are marvelous "come-ons" invented by God to get the job done. Sexual joys are among the body's best and they, too, are purposeful. They are divided into primary joys and secondary joys. The primary sexual joys are the free-flowing, spontaneous reactions of body and mind and are not sinful. The secondary sexual joys are the deliberately stimulated reactions of body and mind and are confined to the pledgees of the marriage contract who have earned this personal "thank you" from God.

CHAPTER IV

Masturbation (Part I)

1. INTRODUCTION

What is masturbation? A Professor Campbell who has done a lot of research in the area of sex defines masturbation as "a direct self-manipulation of the genitals, most commonly by the hand, accompanied by fantasies that are usually of a recognizably sexual nature and having as its aim the discharge of sexual excitation." In every day language, masturbation means playing with one's sexual organs, causing the penis to become erect and finally the seed fluid to spurt out in discharge. Sometimes this is done by hand or other times by the rubbing of the penis against something like the bed sheet. The act of masturbation is often accompanied by thoughts, day dreams or make-believe imaginations about sex. Masturbation, self-abuse, playing with oneself—all are the same thing.

Who masturbates? If you, the reader, do, you may think that you're the only boy who does, but all scientific studies show that masturbation is quite frequent among adolescents. The percentage for boys from ages 13 to 15 goes anywhere from 85 to 96 per cent! Not only that, but it is estimated that a boy between his fourteenth and fifteenth years will masturbate more than any other period of his life and that, roughly, 65 percent practice masturbation for four years. Some boys will masturbate anywhere from three to eight or more times a week. Masturbation is so common that two priests in a book called

53

Counseling the Catholic conclude that "the masturbator is the rule and the abstainer the exception."

At this point (assuming that you're among the majority) I will presume that your thoughts are running something like this: "O.K. I'm not alone. I have a problem and apparently most of my friends do. But what I want to know is *why?* Why is the problem so common. Besides, if practically everybody does it then it's almost normal. How can it be a sin? And anyway, what can a boy do about it?"

Well, that's a lot of questions. To answer them all is going to make this a two chapter response in our book. But they're sincere questions and I will be as honest as I can in answering them, and I will speak more directly and personally to you here than I do elsewhere. Let's take the first question, "Why is masturbation so frequent? Why do so many boys masturbate at one time or another?" Well, there are a lot of answers to this. For one thing, the average boy like yourself gets little or no sex education so he blunders into trouble. Most of the good kids I know stumbled into masturbation and by the time they realized that it was wrong, they were hooked. I said you get no sex education. That's not quite correct. You constantly get the wrong education—from *Playboy,* the movies, TV, etc. as we indicated in the last chapter. But I mean *real* education telling you what sex is really about. No doubt you wonder about sex, talk about sex and even drool about sex, but chances are you have never really thought about sex, about your body and why you're getting a "new" one during adolescence and just what God has to say about you and sex. This book is trying to fill you in on these areas but how many boys will this book reach? Such lack of knowledge and understanding about sex is fairly common, so we can put down ignorance as one factor in the masturbation problem.

But there are other reasons why a boy masturbates, reasons that may be a little deep but are worth investigating. For one thing, doctors tell us that masturbation is very often a psychological problem. By that they mean that masturbation is more often a symptom than the disease. You should know the difference between a symptom and a disease: the disease is the sickness itself and the symptom is merely the signal that beeps out clues to the disease. For example, if a man was all yellow the doctor would not treat his skin. Rather, he would know that the yellow skin might be the symptom (outward sign) that the real disease is in the man's liver; he has jaundice. If you blush, it's not that you have complexion trouble, but the blushing (symptom) is the outward sign that somebody said something that bothered you inside.

So, too, with masturbation. It is often an outside signal-symptom of something else inside a person. Take an imaginary Joe. Joe's not too popular. He's a loner. He's not too sharp in school, he can't play sports, he looks like Alfred E. Newman and—let's really lay it on—he has bad breath! Joe obviously has lots of problems. He has lots of problems *inside;* he feels bad. He could compensate for all his defects by doing something well, like fooling around with car motors or something like that, but he doesn't. Joe is a prime victim for masturbation. He'll probably masturbate many times a week and he'll do it, not because he consciously wants to (like you he feels guilty and ashamed each time), but because unconsciously masturbation represents a temporary forgetfulness and a suspension from his other real problems. If Joe ever brought this problem to the priest, in a short time the priest would see the situation and he would not waste his time concentrating on the "sin" of masturbation, but in trying to help Joe in his other problems inside. As Joe comes to terms with them (the disease) the masturbation (the symptom) will let up.

I would again point out to you that Joe's masturbation was not done on purpose. As I said, Joe feels rotten each time he does it. He doesn't realize that unconsciously, underneath, he's taking his problems out on himself—which is not a very constructive thing to do. His masturbating, in his case, is an immature, childish symptom that's hiding the real disease of his personal problems. Like many boys (like yourself?) Joe is simply not coming to terms with growing up and with his developing personality. I mentioned that this is what the doctors say about many boys' masturbation problem. Just for the record let me quote several of these doctors and psychiatrists and let them express their own words about this aspect of the problem.

In his book, *Healthy Attitudes Towards Love and Sex,* Dr. C. J. Trimbos writes:

> Self-abuse, or masturbation as it is often called, is a very common expression of immature, undeveloped and cramped sexuality. . . . How does it come about that by far the majority of those who do practice self-abuse have a painful feeling of guilt about it . . . (a feeling) just as widespread among non-Christians. . . . The feeling of guilt and discomfort is related to the significance a man attaches to his manliness. As natural as it is for a child to be completely absorbed in itself, in its own body, in playing with his hands and feet and in its own sexual or-

gans, for adults the same thing would be unnatural, immature and inhibited.

> . . . Self-abuse makes us aware of our lack of freedom, our immaturity, our inadequacy. . . . Self-abuse breaks the bonds of our common humanity. It is voluntary loneliness and isolation. It is a secret act. Self-abuse is the expression of unwillingness, or rather—as it is in most cases—the inability to rise above oneself and one's own egotistical demands to a surrender in love. . . . Self-abuse is more of a symptom, as the result of something that lies deeper, of a not entirely successful adjustment to life. Thus masturbation is often not a cause but an effect. . . .[2]

Dr. Alexander A. Schneiders, in his book, *Adolescents and the Challenge of Maturity* admits that

> . . . Sexual impulses and inclinations disturb and frighten the adolescent because they seem to be so powerful and so easily get out of hand. . . . This causes the youngster considerable anxiety and . . . this feeling is strongly reinforced by actual behavior, particularly masturbation because he finds it so difficult to avoid repetition. . . . Parents should be aware that masturbation itself will not lead to physical damage as was thought at one time. The trouble with it, rather, is that it is an immature and maladjustive type of response, it is immoral and it tends to impair the young man's image of himself and even to alienate him from the society of his peers. . . ."[3]

In his other book, *Personality Development and Adjustment in Adolescence* Dr. Schneiders warns that

> . . . Masturbation produces serious psychological and social aftermaths that can be very damaging to healthy development and wholesome adjustment . . . and preoccu-

pation with the problem consumes much energy. . . .
Perhaps its worst feature, psychologically, is that it is a
decidedly immature response . . . (but) when satisfac-
tory emotional outlets are available the child who experiments with masturbation does not usually carry it to extremes and repeats it only occasionally.[4]

Notice, this was the problem with our friend Joe. His
masturbation, as I pointed out, was an immature response to his real problems and if he could only find better outlets to express his personality, his problem would
lessen. (Again, there may be a clue for you here.) A Dr.
John A. Schindler, in his book, *How to Live 365 Days a
Year* puts the matter briefly by saying that

. . . Masturbating causes the individual to withdraw into
himself and into a dream world of his own making. . . .
To put it simply—masturbation is immaturity. It is a
childish way of satisfying one of the basic needs. Just as
with other forms of immaturity it is bound to be unsuc-
cessful in a world which calls for maturity.[5]

And a man named Von Gagern who has done a lot of
study in this field likewise categorizes masturbation as a
"symptom of the individual who cannot deal adequately
with himself, and with life and the world in general; he is
in a state of psychic disorder."

Well, all this comes back to trying to answer your
question, "Why do so many boys masturbate?" One of
the answers is that it's not because the boy is bad or
really wants to do it; his masturbating is often a symptom, a signal that he's not solving the real problems of
growing up. Since nobody's perfect and since adolescence
is by definition a shaky transition time it's not surprising
that the problem is persistent during these years. (At this

point you might want to put this book down and take a good look inside yourself and ask yourself what's *really* bothering you, a question I'll ask you later on.)

Finally, I want to give one more answer to your question about the frequency of the problem. I refer to the natural "tension" difficulty. The tension—which is more of a problem for you than it was for me in my day—is the strain between growing up biologically early and growing up emotionally late. You boys grow up physically earlier these days than twenty or thirty years ago. Must be all those vitamins you get. Anyway, twenty or thirty years ago most boys would start to mature sexually, get their first hair around their penis and under their arms and show other signs of physical development around the late eighth, ninth or tenth grades. Nowadays there are several boys in our school who have the same signs in the sixth grade! Most "arrive" by the seventh and eighth grades. Now this wouldn't necessarily be so bad but today in our society you've got to go to school longer and longer. This means that you've got to depend on your family longer and delay your taking on responsibilities and decisions and marriage. You are kept emotionally immature longer. So, it comes down to the "tension" difficulty: you're getting your sexual drives earlier and your emotional ability to handle them later! And this, too, accounts for the abuse of masturbation.

All right. Before I give a summary of this part let me take a final shot at your other remark at the beginning about if everybody's (almost) doing it, it must be normal so how can it be wrong? Ah, but here (I reply) you're confusing standards with percentages. Perhaps an example will help. Doctors report that a large percentage of the populace catches a cold; in fact, it's labeled the "common" cold for just that reason. Now this high percentage is not going to lead some doctor to declare that the common cold is a standard of health. No, a cold is medically bad. Most people catch one through carelessness, not taking care of themselves, running out without the proper clothing, etc. They raise the percentage for all these reasons, but the standard of health is still the absence of the common cold. The same applies to masturbation. Most boys fall into it because of carelessness, ignorance, through the normal stumbling into adulthood. Still, it's a defect and by no means should it be the standard of emotional or spiritual health. Like the cold, masturbation is normal in the sense of "common" but not normal in the sense of right.

Let us summarize what we've learned so far before we go onto the next part:

1. Masturbation is a very frequent and common problem among adolescent boys.
2. The causes are varied: we mentioned first, ignorance about sex and growing up as one of them.
3. Next, masturbation may also be, and frequently is, a symptom, a sign on the outside that a boy is not coming to terms with his inside problems of personality. Since adolescence is by nature a stress time of personality transition it is not surprising that the problem of masturbation is most frequent at this period.
4. Also, an added pressure to make masturbation a problem for a boy is his earlier sexual physical development and his later emotional independence. In other words, he gets his strong drives earlier and his ability to control them later.
5. Finally, other factors in the problem are, of course, a

boy's own weaknesses, his flirting with temptation, his built-in Original Sin tendencies.

6. In any case, masturbation is, as the doctors tell us, a really immature response to life and caters to an already existing selfishness and self-centeredness that none of us can afford to increase.

7. Therefore, to control this problem is highly desirable in developing a well balanced and manly personality. The problem must be dealt with and overcome.

2. SERIOUS MATTER, SIN AND "GOOD WILL"

Now that we have some insights into the masturbation problem let's move into the more personal moral area where we're going to ask whether masturbation is a sin and get some surprising answers.

We must begin our investigation by getting some careful distinctions which will help you a great deal in solving our question. I'll begin by asking you a question: "What are the three things necessary to make a sin mortal?" If you remembered your catechism or ran and looked it up you will tell me that the three things necessary to make a sin mortal are:

a) serious matter
b) sufficient knowledge both that something is serious and you know what you're doing
c) full and final consent of the will

Now, let us pause right here and take a second look and note that there are *three* ingredients to a mortal sin and these three ingredients must be taken altogether if the end product is to be a sin. I emphasize this because most of you say the words, "serious matter," stop right there and immediately jump to "sin." *But this is wrong!*

Serious matter alone does not equal sin, but serious matter PLUS the other two points of knowledge and full consent equal sin. Therefore, something can be a serious matter but not necessarily a sin! Sin is the result of all three points not the result of merely one. Let's spend more time on this.

We will describe "serious matter" as the "out-there" object apart from anybody and "sin" as the "inside-involvement" of a person. Now there can be serious matter without your cooperation but unless *you're* involved you can't have any sin. Not only that, unless you're fully and deeply involved you can't have mortal sin. An example may help. Killing a person—this is a serious matter. "Out-there," looking at it in itself, killing a person is a serious matter. Agreed. But suppose the person who did the killing was sleep walking and in his sleep killed someone? Is this "serious matter" a *sin?* Does this sleep-walking murder represent a real "inside-involvement" an in-the-heart-and-mind involvement of the one who did it? You tell me "no" and you're right. The serious matter turns into sin *only* and *if* the subject is consciously and knowingly and intelligently involved. In our case the subject obviously wasn't involved at all. In fact, he was asleep! He neither knew what he was doing nor gave full consent. Look, the point I want to make, once more, is this: you can have a serious matter but not necessarily sin. I repeat: you can never have a sin unless the subject, the person, *you* are involved. That's why you can't commit sin by accident. That's a contradiction. If it's an accident, then, by definition, you neither knew nor wanted something to happen. You can commit a serious matter by accident—such as accidentally running over a person, dropping a hammer from the roof killing the fuller-brush salesman, missing Mass on Sunday when you thought it was Saturday—but you can't commit a sin (which is deliberate) by accident (which is indeliberate). So, something can be serious but *we never talk of sin unless we look to the person who's involved,* his realization, his intention, his understanding, his consent.

Now, how about masturbation? Well, it should be clear by now that we have two questions to ask about it which are quite distinct. Question number one: Is masturbation a serious matter? The answer is yes it is. It is because it involves serious things: The secondary joys of sex, your personality development, your capacity to love, your respect for the sources of human life. Excessive masturbation can make you self-centered, egotistical, ingrown. So we say that we are dealing with a serious matter here.

Now, question number two: Is masturbation a sin? At this point (I hope) you should be able to answer, "It all depends." The answer is "yes" if the person knew it and gave consent, an indication of which is his general carelessness about his spiritual life. But, on the other hand, the answer is "no" if the boy didn't know what he was doing or did not really give his full consent, *an indication of which is his carefulness and sincerity in his spiritual life, his display of general good will.*

Notice the wording I used, "general carefulness and sincerity in his spiritual life" and "display of general good will." Such phrases are most assuredly a background against which to judge the finality of full consent. Generally and obviously a boy can't be very sincere, try real hard to live a pure and good life, pray, fulfill his religious obligations and still give full consent to mortal sin in the matter of masturbation. Such a basic and overall relationship with God in every way is not going to be profoundly and deliberately broken several times a week! In other words, (to get back to you) when it comes to judging yourself and examining yourself on your guilt about masturbation you have to look not only at the individual act to see if you gave full consent, but also to your overall direction in your relationship to God, your constant desire to be pleasing to Him, the general tenor of your approach to Him, your good will. The individual act of masturbation should not be isolated but must be seen in the context of your overall spiritual life. *If this overall spiritual life is generally good and wholesome, then it can be safely assumed that full consent is not present and you are not guilty of mortal sin even though you did something which is called serious matter.* To put it more simply, whether you personally are guilty of the *sin* of masturbation depends largely on whether or not you are a boy of "Good Will."

The point to make now, of course, is to find out if you *are* such a boy of Good Will. This is not as hard as it sounds. If you can sincerely answer "Yes" to the following five questions, you are a boy of "Good Will":

1) Do I go to church regularly?
2) Do I pray, especially in time of temptation?
3) Do I go to confession and communion regularly —at least every month or two?
4) Do I follow the advice of the priest in confession if and when he speaks to me on this problem?
5) Do I avoid the real voluntary and dangerous oc-

casions of sin: the people, the places, the books
and magazines that give me a hard time?

If you can answer all of these questions truthfully in
the affirmative, then you are a boy of Good Will and it is
most likely that, even though you may fall into the serious matter of masturbation, you are not guilty of the *sin*
of masturbation. True, individual acts of masturbation
can, on occasion, be deliberate, can be on purpose—but
this is not likely in general. No boy can faithfully answer
"yes" to the five questions and at the same time be deliberately breaking his relationship with the God he loves
so much. So, let me again repeat the conclusion to our
question, "Is masturbation a sin?" The answer is "No, not
for the boy of Good Will." However, if you're unsure of
yourself or think you're letting yourself off too lightly,
feel free to talk to the priest about it in confession (more
on this later) to back up your stand. But, on the other
hand, don't be afraid to trust your own judgment and if
the answers to the five questions really are affirmative—
especially number 2 where you prayed when you were
having the problem—then you know you are not guilty
of sin.

Before I leave this part I want to raise one final important and sensitive question that flows from what I've said
above. May a boy who is having a masturbation problem
go to communion without first going to confession? The
answer once more is, "Yes—for the boy of Good Will."
Let me here quote directly from a well known and kindly
moralist, Father Bernard Haring. In his book on confession called *Shalom* he says

> The question is often asked: should the confessor allow
> such penitents who have not yet overcome the masturba-

tion problem to go to communion without previous confession? The answer depends on the penitent's moral level, on the measure of his good will and on the effects of such a permission. It happens at times that boys and girls want to go to communion because of the need to conform to the community pattern of family that receives regularly. However, many adolescents resist conformity on this point and wish to receive communion because of the meaning it has for them; the intention is sincere. Then it is a question of knowing whether they have the necessary good will. Are they striving to gain complete control of themselves? If they display good will by accepting the few remedies prescribed for them by the confessor, he can presume that they are generally of good will and he can tell them something like this: "By divine law and the law of the Church we must go to confession before communion only if we are morally certain that we have committed a mortal sin. In your case, however, since you are so young and show so much good will, I would not dare to presume that you had committed a mortal sin. We can leave the judgment in this matter to God. Make an act of contrition and an act of confidence whenever you fall, and repeat these acts before going to communion; then tell me about your progress in fraternal love and on this point in the next confession." (p. 198)[6]

Notice how often Father Haring mentions good will and puts the emphasis on sincerity and struggle. You see once more how much depends on your good will and that if you're really trying and there's genuine love in your heart then the good God will even keep the door of Holy Communion open to you. Talk this over with a priest if you wish and your good will, if proven and demonstrated, can win this same approach to frequent communion for you.

CHAPTER V

Masturbation (Part II)

1. MORAL GUIDELINES

In this chapter I am going to summarize the moral principles of the three previous chapters with special application to and advice on the masturbation problem. Also I will give you actual confessional cases but I would emphasize that in every instance I have the full permission from the boys involved (all my friends and penitents) to recount them.

1. *Indeliberate arousal is never a sin.* Another way to express the same principle is: *The primary joys of sex are never sinful.* Let's give several examples showing, once more, that serious-matter events such as sexual arousal are not the same thing as sin. A boy is walking down the street and suddenly a bee comes along and stings him on the arm. Is this a serious matter? Sure is! He might get infected and very ill from it. Does he know he's been stung? Yes, that's why he's yelling like mad all over the street. But did he will this, want it, was he "involved" in having this happen? Of course not! He's a normal boy and is simply a victim of what the psychologists call the S-R, the Stimulus-Response pattern. The bee sting was the Stimulus and he, being equipped with nerve endings in his skin, gave the Response (a yell). God made him and every other human being that way.

Take another boy going down the street. He's just come from his doctor who's told him that he has some in-

67

crease in sugar in his blood and he'll have to lay off sweets for six months. On his way home he passes Mrs. Jones' house and on her window sill is an apple pie which he loves. The pie—here, the Stimulus—sets up a Response: he begins to drool as his saliva glands automatically begin to react. The whole experience is very pleasant, a primary joy. The boy enjoys the smell of the pie, the mouth-watering and even the stomach noises that just started. He'd certainly like to have the pie, but he's a good boy, won't steal it and besides he shouldn't take any sweets on his doctor's orders. There was a serious matter here: his health and possible stealing. The boy knew it but he wouldn't consent to theft or the risk of bad health.

All right, now let's take the matter of sexual arousal. Jack is fifteen. He's walking down the street also and comes upon one of those sexy movie ad signs with an attractive girl on it wearing practically nothing but a smile. She is a Stimulus, that's for sure. Jack, being normal and equipped by God with nerve endings, gives a Response. In this case he gets the sexy image fantasy going in his mind. It's pleasant and enjoyable and he begins to feel a sensation in his penis and the penis even begins to harden as his erection begins. Sin? No, no more than there is sin in yelling from the bee sting or mouth-watering at the apple pie. All three—yelling, mouth-watering and erecting—are built-in, God-given Responses to Stimuli. They are indeliberate, automatic, mechanical arousals that may be concerned about serious matters—possible infection, sugar diabetes, purity—but none can be sins because there was no "inside involvement" or deliberateness on the part of the boys. And just because two of these experiences dealt with the primary joys of sex—the pie and the sexy picture—that's still no reason to suspect sin. We saw in a previous chapter that such primary sexual joys belong to the adolescent boy and primary sexual joys are never sins. Nor will they ever be as long as a boy doesn't stop, shift gears as it were into the secondary sexual joys and willfully and deliberately change what is indeliberate to something on purpose.

Two more common examples of this principle which we gave before: the wet dream. The dream (Stimulus) becomes so strong that it causes a Reponse (release of the seed fluid). Sin? How could there be? True, the matter at hand is serious but the whole arousal was entirely indeliberate; there was no consent, no knowledge and no personal "inside involvement." Just a free, spontaneous primary joy of sex. Or the erection again. Some guys are so excitable that they have an erection every time some pretty girl passes by. No problem. Like the wet dream an erection is merely a primary sexual Response to any kind of proper Stimulus. You're conscious it's happening, you acknowledge the excitement but you don't deliberately want to offend your own dignity or God's law.

Take Bob: He comes to confession and says something like this to me:

Bob: Father, it's Bob. Father, you know how narrow our hallways are in school?

Father: Yes, Bob.

Bob: Well, every once in a while, while we're changing classes the crowd is so tight that some girl presses against me. Well, I get sort of all worked up, you know. . . .

Father: You mean, you have an erection?

Bob: Yeah. And then I'm stuck with it the rest of the

period. If I stand up in class I have to hold a book in front of me!

Father: (Here I have to give a chuckle because I can just see Bob sweating it out!) All right, Bob; but, come on, are you asking me about sin here? You know the answer. You're a boy of Good Will and that's why you're here. You make your own judgment.

After a few exchanges like that Bob reasserted his own good judgment and correctly concluded he committed no sin. He even remembered the principle, "Indeliberate arousal is never a sin" and that he simply got the free bonus of a primary sexual joy!

2. *Struggle is not sin.* This is a fine principle and simply states in other terms what I've said before. An illustration from the confessional will best explain it.

Joe: Bless me, Father, for I have sinned. Father this is Joe. It's one month since my last confession. I told a few lies, was distracted in my prayers, had a fight with my sister and I masturbated five times.

Father: Joe, about this masturbation, did you just do it or what?

Joe: No, Father. I was in bed and a few times I touched myself. Then I took my hand away. Then I started again and then. . . .

Father: Joe, did you pray at these times?

Joe: Oh, yes, Father, I even got up and went to the kitchen to get some milk to try to stop—but I wound up doing it anyway. . . .

Father: Joe, what principle I taught you should cover these cases and help you to form your conscience?

Joe: You mean the "Struggle is not sin" one?

Father: Yes. (There's a pause here while Joe thinks it over.) Well, Joe, what do you say?

Joe: Well, Father, I really did try. I did struggle. I guess those five times weren't sins.

Father: That's right, Joe. They weren't. Although it's always good for you to recount them to me here just for the sake of testing your own judgment and letting me see how you're assessing your spiritual development.

Get the principle? Struggle is not sin for the simple reason that any struggle indicates lack of *full* consent of the will. How can a person struggle and still give full consent? To my way of thinking, prayer is always an excellent clue that as a matter of fact struggle took place. That's why I asked Joe immediately if he prayed in the time of his temptation. His "yes" answer told me of his lack of full consent. Besides, Joe is one of those boys of Good Will and I knew on that account also that his serious matter problem was not a sin for him. Remember, than, even if, like Joe, you wind up masturbating after all (serious matter) there is not sin if you have Good Will and struggle is surely such a sign.

3. *Doubtful sins are not sins.* This principle is again illustrated by a real case. Ken, let's call him, wakes up on Sunday and he can see from his starchy pajamas and bed sheet that his seed fluid was expelled during the night. He also remembers vaguely that he did wake up and started to masturbate himself. He stopped and started several times. He was half asleep, may have mumbled a prayer. Anyway, sitting on the edge of his bed this Sunday morning he's not sure and he's wondering if he should go to Holy Communion. Ken has a doubt. If he remembers this principle that doubtful sins are not sins then Ken can resolve his problem and go to Communion when he attends Mass.

These three principles (1) Indeliberate arousal is
never a sin (2) Struggle is not sin and (3) Doubtful sins
are not sins—all are variations of what I have been trying
to say about the primary sexual joys in general and the
masturbation problem in particular. Masturbation, like
most matters of sex, involves serious matter, but is not
too often a question of sin for the boy of Good Will. If he
stays loose, tries to come to terms with his body and its
functions and reactions (S-R), if he is really trying
(Struggle) and knows that sin must be a pretty sure thing
(Doubt) then he has much more of a leeway in making
his judgments than he thought. As I said earlier, he simply can't be breaking in a profound way his whole relationship with God three or four times a week when everything else in his life—his Mass, his prayer life, his charity, his frequent confessions and communions, his efforts
to avoid the occasions of sin—all tell precisely the opposite story: That he has a good relationship with God,
loves Him and wants to give his whole heart and soul to
Him!

Does all this mean that no boy can commit the sin of
masturbation and willfully and deliberately steal the secondary joys of sex but just fall into the serious matter of
masturbation? By no means. Pius XII reminded us that
the sin is quite possible for an adolescent. Boys who don't
care, who are careless about Mass, hardly ever go to the
sacraments, flirt with sexy magazines and evil-talking companions are building a dangerous pattern of irreligious
lives, a context that does *not* show good will and they can
and do commit sin. Even the boy of Good Will, on occasion, can be careless and give in to the sin. But, generally,
if he is what we have described as the boy of Good Will,

the chances are greatly in his favor that he does not sin when he has trouble with the serious matter of masturbation.

2. SOME ADVICE AND WARNINGS

In this part I want to zero in on some particulars that will help you in the fight for control in overcoming the masturbation problem:

1. *Be positive about sex.* The first piece of advice I would give you is to learn about sex, as much as you can. Not, as I said before, from the street or your own companions, but from a good and reliable source. Your parish priest is usually a good help here. So are some pamphlets and books and so I've mentioned some of the better ones for you in a list at the end. But do think well of sex in spite of all the exploitation and nonsense shoved at you by adults who never grew up. Remember man connected sin and guilt with sex; God had nothing but dignity and joy and openness in mind when He invented it. Be proud of your body no matter what condition it's in. You need your body. It's your "sacrament," your "instrument," your "outward sign" by which you do things and worship and make love and play and run and jump and drive a car. Don't knock your body. Be positive.

2. *Beware of excessive masturbation.* If you're masturbating five or more times a week over a period of time, this certainly is a sign that you've got problems elsewhere. Remember all the quotes from the doctors? Maybe it's time to take a good look at yourself in the mirror. O.K.—after you've screamed, take a closer look—but inside yourself. What's really bothering you? School? marks? getting along with girls? undersized? your father's

an alcoholic or your parents are separated? you're too tall
or too short, big ears or big nose? jealous of your brother
or sister or the popular kid in school? But what exactly
are you doing to improve yourself and overcome these
problems? If you're just moping around feeling sorry for
yourself, no wonder you have a masturbation problem. If
you can't work out your problems by yourself, seek someone who can help you. Remember too that even infre-
quent masturbation is undesirable and is a challenge that
must be met.

3. *Beware of fixation.* This hurts a lot of guys! How
many good kids waste a terrible amount of energy worrying about sex and their masturbation problem! It's like
one of those Charlie Brown episodes where Linus is concentrating on his tongue. Lucy, of course, tells him he's
out of his mind but by the time the end of the strip comes
Lucy has become acutely aware of *her* tongue and it's
driving her nuts. Well, it's true; the more you think about
and worry about masturbation the more its on your mind
and the more you're going to do it. Another result of feeling so darn guilty all the time and worrying all the time
about it is that you let every other good point you have
go by the board. You're giving the impression that the
only virtue in the world is chastity. Well, I've got news
for you. Chastity is about 86th down the line. Which is
an exaggerated way of saying that *Charity* is the queen of
all virtues and chastity is only a variety of charity. You
do ninety-nine things right, have all kinds of good points
to develop and expand and then you go wasting your
time worrying over the masturbation problem and not
taking the other opportunities to grow in charity. That fixation business is bad. The best thing for you is to go out
and try to be friendly and helpful to others, to practice

charity and get out of yourself for a while. All right, so you've got a problem. How much of the day does it take up, for heaven's sake! Spend the rest of your time figuring how to help others or work on your hobby or shoot a few baskets and get started on some project. The less time spent on worrying on one fixed point, the better all the way around.

The priest often takes this tactic with the good boy; that is, not spending too much time on the masturbation problem but getting the boy to work on something else. At first this puzzles and sometimes upsets a boy. Consider Mike who later told me his reaction. Mike's confession went something like this:

Mike: Bless me, Father. It's Mike, Father. I've been sassing back my mother a few times and I told a few lies. It's been a month since my last confession and I've masturbated fifteen times.

Father: What about your prayer life during this time, Mike? And your promise to do something kind for your little sister?

Mike: I've really been praying, Father, especially with all my—trouble. I took my little sister to the movies once, but I haven't really been that nice to her the rest of the time. . . .

Father: I see. Well, Mike, why don't you shoot for just something nice—something you don't really have to do—for one member of your family each week. And try saving a dime a week and when you come back for your confession next time put whatever you've saved into the poor box, O.K.? Now, for your penance just go out and kneel in the pew for a few minutes looking up at the crucifix and just tell Jesus how much you love Him.

Later Mike told me that he was surprised and a little upset that I showed so little shock or concern about his masturbation problem. Instead I went off about his little sister and so forth. As time went on, though, Mike began to see the wisdom of what I was trying to do with him. After all, I know Mike. He's a kid of "Good Will." I know he's trying and that he's bugged about his problem. I've talked to him before about it in confession and I'll talk to him again. But I don't want to overemphasize it and I felt that Mike was getting too hung up on it. In the long run Mike has profited from my urging him to turn away from exclusive preoccupation with this one problem to working on his giving and loving capacity for others. So, it comes down to this. Fixation's a bad thing. There's a lot of other ways of being a good christian in this world besides just worrying about sex!

4. *Practice charity*. This is a further emphasis of what I've said. Charity is the main virtue. Develop your friendships for example. Call up your buddy and ask what *he* wants to do tonight. See if you can help your teacher after school. Do something for your Mom or Dad without being asked. Drop a few pennies into the poor box. Develop a hobby. See if you can get involved in any of your community's social affairs, project "Head Start" and that sort of thing. The point is always the same: charity is love, masturbation basically is self-love. You'll only cancel the one by doing the other.

5. *Get in touch with a priest*. This bit of advice may seem the hardest. After all, maybe the priest knows you outside of confession. Maybe he thinks you're a great guy and now you're going to go up to him and say, "Hey, Father, you know what? I masturbate!" Then, of course,

he'll fall back from shock and your picture will be in next Sunday's bulletin with the caption, "Public Sinner No. 1." Well, I promise you it won't be as crude as that. If you ever did say such a thing ten to one the priest's reply will be, "I know it. Glad you brought it up. Want me to help you?" Look, the priest knows what boys are made of. He was a boy himself and he had to meet the same challenge. You'll find him sympathetic and helpful. If you want, he'll work with you both inside and outside the confessional. He can guide you on the spot, help you to form a mature conscience, sharpen your judgments and even help you to more frequent communion. You'll find having a friend in your priest and confiding in him one of the shortest cuts in overcoming the problem. If you're really too embarrassed to confront your priest openly, then ask him about it in confession and go back to him all the time. Use a code name if you wish, but keep in contact.

6. *Be prepared for the "slump" problem.* The "slump" problem means that no matter what a boy does, no matter how hard he tries, he just can't seem to get out of the rut or slump of masturbating. There was a time when he was doing fairly well, but every once in a while he gets in a slump and nothing will help. He struggles, he prays, he pleads with God, he goes to the sacraments. But not only is he not getting better, he's getting worse! Indeed, he is in a real slump. The great tendency is going to be to get discouraged and maybe even stop going to confession (exactly what the devil wants. What a victory if he swings this!) All that I can tell you is that this problem is not unlike the slump problem of the big league batter. He goes into a batting slump and nothing he seems to do works out. His manager has learned to have patience with

him and knows from experience that he'll just have to
wait it out. The same with you. Don't ever get so discouraged that you make a decision to keep away from God.
Just ride it out. In fact, I usually tell the boys who are
experiencing this to go a step further and to offer their
slump periods to God. Not that I'm saying to offer sins to
God, but to offer up to Him the whole humiliating cross.
Say a prayer like this, "Dear Jesus, the only thing I have
left to give you is this problem which is driving me crazy.
It's about the only thing that's really mine and so here it
is: the problem, the struggle, the anger I feel, the frustration I feel, the shame I feel—I give it all to you as my
sacrifice!" I bet there's seldom a more fervent and acceptable teen-age prayer than that!

This brings up, by the way, an interesting side comment a boy once put to me. "Father, purity is good,
right? I pray for it and beg for it. Why, then, doesn't God
give me something which is so obviously worthwhile?" A
good question. Remember that I kiddingly said that chastity is 86th down the line in the list of virtues? By that I
meant that purity isn't the greatest teenage virtue or any
one else's for that matter. Charity is primary and other
virtues, too, are important, like courage and manliness
and perseverance. What I'm driving at is that God could
give you an "instant cure" and from that moment on you
would be absolutely pure. But would you be a man for
having something handed to you like that? In this life you
have to prove yourself to God. That's why we're here.
Proving means that you'll be tested. So God tests you, lets
you sweat it out, gives you the opportunity to develop
spiritual guts. He's teaching you in your young life the
virtue of perseverance. The way you struggle now, the

way you stick with it now is the way you'll perform as a
grown man. If you simply throw in the towel, give up,
surrender to despair, drop off going to the sacraments,
bow to discouragement, you'll never be a man. No, you
must stick with it and God is not going to hear your
prayer for an instant cure because He's training you to
other virtues. After your hard time has passed, you'll
emerge a stronger man and a better christian risk for the
future. What God in His goodness has done, you see, is to
give you something greater than purity. He's given you
the opportunity to grow in character. A wise and gentle
Anglican christian man, C. S. Lewis put it this way several years ago. He said in his fine little book called *Mere
Christianity* (italics mine):

> We may, indeed, be sure that perfect chastity—like per-
> fect charity—will not be attained by any merely human
> efforts. You must ask for God's help. Even when you
> have done so, it may seem that no help, or less help than
> you need, is being given. Never mind. After each failure,
> ask forgiveness, pick yourself up, and try again. Very
> often, what God first helps us towards is not the virtue
> itself *but just this power of trying again.* For however
> important chastity (or courage or truthfulness, or any
> other virtue) may be, this process trains us in habits of
> the soul *which are more important still.*[7]

So, we come back to my original advice: don't let the
"slump" problem get you down. It may be a sign that, in
the long run, God is at work making a man out of you!

7. *Walk first, run later.* This thought flows from the
one we've just talked about and is something Jesus taught
us; but, to be frank, it's a concept which I find your age
group has a real blind spot about. This principle of Grad-

ualness, as we may call it, simply states that it takes time to become a man, a saint. Like we said above, there are no instant cures. Now, if you think about it, you readily accept this principle when applied to everything whatsoever in your life—but not as regards virtue! You expect, for example, to continue schooling because you know you can't get everything the first time around. You've got to take your education step by step—gradually, and you're quite prepared for a long run. Or you're not growing up over night. You didn't go to bed one night with an eight year old body and wake up the next morning with the body you have now. Growing takes time. It's a process. If you want to be a baseball pitcher or basketball star there's lots of practice and trial and error in store for you since you're not going to catch on immediately. As I say, you easily accept all of this. Yet, you and your friends have a real blind spot when it comes to purity and manly character. You really *do* want an instant cure. You'd like to go to confession, tell your sins and on your way out say to the priest, "Thanks, Father, that takes care of that. No more temptations, no more trouble with purity!" Somehow you have a hard time in accepting that virtue, like education and physical growth and athletic proficiency, doesn't come easy and you're going to have a lot of sexual ups and downs before you can make that statement to Father—if ever! No, Jesus taught us that spiritual growth is like a mustard seed. It's the smallest seed but grows into one of the largest trees. And it doesn't happen like it does on the TV cartoons. You drop the seed into the ground and you have to jump back because the tree zaps right past you into the sky! That's make-believe. In real life it may take that seed twenty or thirty years or more to develop into a mature tree. The seed of grace is like that. It will grow *gradually* in you. You just have to water it constantly with charity, prayer and your liturgical life of Mass, confession and communion. With purity, as with any other virtue, there are no instant cures.

8. *Keep a sense of humor*. Don't be so serious about your problem! I'm not saying that it's not serious but have confidence in God and your own Good Will—and smile. I'd like to see you get a nice healthy sense of humor about yourself and about sex—to be able to laugh at the things Jesus would laugh at, to appreciate girls, to nod understandingly at the reactions of your own body. Enjoy being a boy and keep a sense of humor.

Let's now pull into an outline summary the main points of the last two chapters:

1. Masturbation is a very frequent problem among growing boys.
2. One cause is ignorance: the average boy doesn't understand sex or his own growing up process.
3. Another cause is a boy's failure to work out other personal problems in his life and masturbation becomes a constant symptom of this condition.
4. Another cause is that today's boys grow up physically and sexually earlier but their emotional ability to control themselves comes later.
5. Other causes would include the strong allurements of the world and the boy's own built-in Original Sin weakness.
6. Masturbation is a serious matter, but whether it's a sin is another question.
7. The general presumption is, that for a boy of Good Will, masturbation is seldom a sin.
8. His "Good Will" condition is tested by his fidelity to his liturgical and prayer life.

9. Such a "Good Will" boy may have access to Communion without prior confession.
10. Indeliberate responses to stimuli, struggles, doubtful sins —all fit into the same general pattern and are not sins.
11. A boy is urged to be positive about sex, practice charity and keep his humor in his struggles.
12. But be careful of excessive masturbation, a fixation problem, the "slump" problem and bring your problem to your parish priest.

CHAPTER VI

Sin and Confession

1. LUST AND GUILT

Mrs. Foster raised her hand at one of our parents' sessions on sex education. "Father, I don't see why we should talk of sin to our youngsters. We don't want to give them a guilt complex and make them feel there's something wrong or evil about sex. Sex should be a healthy and normal part of their lives. They shouldn't be afraid of it."

Mrs. Foster is right—and she is wrong. Yes, sex should be a healthy part of your lives. We've tried to be honest with you even to the point of bluntness about the use of sex and its wonderful joys. We've tried to show that there is not as much sin connected with sex as you might have thought; that as it comes from the hand of God there is no sin connected with sex. Here Mrs. Foster is right. But she's forgetting that the gift is given to *man*, not angels. Man, unfortunately, is quite capable of taking something very beautiful and distorting it and misusing it and in the real world this does happen. Even the boy of good will is capable of lust or the misuse of sex; even he is capable of stealing the secondary joys of sex without the attendant responsibilities. Not to admit this, not to speak of sin, is to be unreal.

It wasn't always so though. I mean, there was a time when even man did not attach sin to sex. In fact, we can pinpoint the time in history when man acquired his built-

83

in weakness about sex. That time goes back to the dawn
of mankind itself. The Bible tells us about it. The perti-
nent and far-reaching event is recorded in Genesis 2:21:

> Yahweh God said, 'It is not good that man should be
> alone. I will make him a helpmate . . . So Yahweh God
> made the man fall into a deep sleep. And while he slept,
> he took one of his ribs and enclosed it in flesh. Yahweh
> God built the rib he had taken from the man into a
> woman and brought her to the man . . . Now both of
> them were naked, the man and his wife, but they felt no
> shame in front of each other.

> The serpent was the most subtle of all the wild beasts
> that Yahweh God had made. It asked the woman, 'Did
> God really say you were not to eat from any of the trees
> in the garden?' The woman answered the serpent, 'We
> may eat the fruit of the trees in the garden. But of the
> fruit of the tree in the middle of the garden God said
> "You must not eat it, nor touch it, under pain of
> death." ' Then the serpent said to the woman, 'No! You
> will not die! God knows in fact that on the day you eat
> it your eyes will be opened and you will be like gods,
> knowing good and evil.' The woman saw that the tree
> was good to eat and pleasing to the eye, and that it was
> desirable for the knowledge that it could give. So she
> took some of its fruit and ate it. She gave some also to
> her husband who was with her, and he ate it. Then the
> eyes of both of them were opened and they realized that
> they were naked. So they sewed fig-leaves together to
> make themselves loin-cloths.

> The man and his wife heard the sound of Yahweh God
> walking in the garden in the cool of the day and they hid
> from Yahweh God among the trees of the garden. But

Yahweh God called to the man, "Where are you?" he asked. "I heard the sound of you in the garden," he replied, "I was afraid because I was naked, so I hid." "Who told you that you were naked?" he asked.

Now notice several interesting things in this dramatic story: Before their disobedience Adam and Eve went naked in front of one another without shame, embarrassment or temptation. Yet, the first recorded fact after their sin was a realization of their nakedness and the scramble to cover the sexual parts of their bodies. God's question is most touching and most revealing. "Who told you that you were naked?" Almost a sad "where did you get this shame from?" God is saying, "how come, all of a sudden, you're embarrassed, you feel temptation, a loss of control? You weren't embarrassed before running around with nothing on!" What happened with Adam and Eve was that, when they deliberately broke their friendship with the Father, when they rerouted their direct and open lovingness with God to their own selfish interests and pride, they did damage to themselves. No longer fully related to God they sent a tremor into their own bodies and minds from which we haven't recovered to this day since, as their children, we have inherited their condition. Adam and Eve threw themselves out of harmony with their Creator and out of harmony with themselves. The open joy of their naked sex became the closed fear of guilt. "I was afraid because I was naked, so I hid."

Such is the story of how built-in disharmony became a part of man's life. Full control of one's urges, appetites and drives, once Adam's natural equipment, is only a memory and a bit of recorded history. The lack of control is now the reality for mankind—and in all things both big and little. You want a few non-sexual examples? All right. Adam (before the Fall) could take a bag of peanuts, take one, open the shell and eat only one. If he didn't want any more he just wouldn't take another one, such was his control and inner harmony. Not you and I. At least not now. I would take more than one; in fact, I'd take and eat the whole bag. Like that TV advertisement for potato chips, you can't take just one. Adam could take one square off a Hersey bar and if he didn't want any more, such was his harmony, that he wouldn't take another piece. Could you do that? I couldn't. I know I'd wind up eating the whole bar. If Adam wanted just one Martini, that's all he would take. It is obvious today that people who should stop at one, don't. The fully uncontrolled drinker, the alcoholic, will even say with all sincerity as he reaches for another drink, "I really shouldn't!" but he can't keep his hands off it. Well, you get the point. We're in the post-harmony era. We have built-in weakness in all things and especially sexual matters. Our "eyes are open" and they see too much. We get hot and bothered about sex easily. We recognize that not too far below the surface is lurking a distinct tendency to steal the secondary joys of sex. The ancient christian writers had a ten dollar word for this condition of ours: "concupiscence." We call it today "lust." But the definition's the same: the leaning to *irresponsible* pleasure. Without understanding this background a boy sometimes wonders about himself, that he's oversexed. He gets so excited about sex. He has a hard time not looking at sexy pictures, of keeping his eyes where they belong and his hands where they belong. Well, in the light of what we have said, he really ought not to think of himself as degenerate or evil. He is simply a victim of Original Sin. He does have a built-in weakness in sexual matters. He can and does sin as a result. Along with the rest of mankind. If it's any comfort, St. Paul publicly complained about his struggles. In Romans 7:18 he writes:

> I cannot understand my own behavior. I fail to carry out the things I want to do, and I find myself doing the very things I hate . . . In fact, this seems to be the rule, that every single time I want to do good it is something evil that comes to hand. In my inmost self I dearly love God's Law, but I see that my body follows a different law that battles against the law which my reason dictates. This is what makes me a prisoner of that law of sin which lives inside my body. What a wretched man I am! Who will rescue me from this body doomed to death?

Today we may laugh when we read that crochety old St. Jerome of the fourth century, when he would get temptations against purity, would roll around naked in thorn bushes! Well, he may have been a little fanatical on the point, but at least he knew he was fighting a passion and that his urges were real and had to be controlled.

Mrs. Foster is not a realist and she simply would not understand St. Jerome. But sin is real and to talk about it to our adolescents is good christian sense. Not, of course, with exaggeration, seeing sin all over the place, but with wisdom and sense and a grasp of reality calling to mind the stern warning of St. Paul in his epistle to the Corinthians (6:9):

> Make no mistake: no fornicator [unmarried people stealing the secondary sexual joys] or idolater, none who are guilty either of adultery or of homosexual perversions,

no thieves, or grabbers or drunkards or slanderers or
swindlers will possess the kingdom of God.

Yes, sin is possible and should be discussed. A boy can:

—willfully and deliberately masturbate himself and
thus take to himself the secondary sexual joys
—willfully and deliberately pause a long time over
sexual thoughts and fantasies to the point of
preoccupation and self-stimulation
—willfully and deliberately touch the sexual areas
of a girl's body and sexually arouse her and himself
beyond the responsibile limits of marriage
—willfully and deliberately have sexual intercourse
with a girl before marriage thus seizing the pleasure but not the purpose

Phyllis McGinley, the Pulitzer Prize winning poet and
wife and mother has this to say about sin in her book,
The Province of the Heart:

Sin has always been an ugly word, but it has been made
so in a new sense over the last half-century. It has been
made not only ugly but passe. People are no longer sinful, they are only immature or underprivileged or frightened or, more particularly, sick. And I think it has no
doubt been helpful to some unfortunates to find themselves so considered. But my daughters and yours are
fairly brave and certainly privileged and more mature
than we might have hoped; and if their souls have been
sick, we should have known it before this. *My* children
would believe themselves morally insulted to have their
misdemeanors classified as illness. In our household we
have never been afraid of sin as a common noun.

So what in the end shall I tell my daughters about chastity before marriage? Of *course,* I shall be sensible and point out the ordinary social penalties attached to any other conduct. I shall touch on the possible pregnancy, the untidyness, and the heartbreak. But I shall also say that love is never merely a biological act but one of the few miracles left on earth, and that to use it cheaply is a sin. In fact that is what I have already told them.[8]

The Catholic boy knows the sense of what this mother is saying.

At this point we are going to add a brief word about a related subject: guilt. I bring this subject up because just as there are people who would do away with all sin (labelling it immaturity or illness as Phyllis McGinley just said), there are those who would deny all guilt. In fact, such people want to do away with sin about sex because it does cause guilt. The answer to this is, "So, what's wrong with guilt?" Guilt is a *normal* consequence for a human being who does wrong. It is healthy because it shows that a person has principles and a sensitivity to wrong doing. A guiltless world would not only be an unreal world, but an unbearably cruel one, a world in which no one could have any honest emotions.

But we must distinguish between two kinds of guilt. There's a destructive guilt and there's a constructive guilt. Destructive guilt is the feeling of deep shame that eats away at a person, leads him to self-pity and may even eventually lead him to self-destruction. It urges him to nothing but to turn in to himself and forget the rest of the world and the kind and merciful people in it. It warps his viewpoint of life. Constructive guilt, on the other hand, is the feeling of shame and self-reproach that leads to repentance, that leads away (not towards) oneself to another. In the case of the moral boy and the christian boy, it leads him to God, to the confessional; it leads him to the feet of Christ Who loves him. The other side of constructive guilt is confidence and trust. In fact, such constructive guilt is helpful in helping a boy to acquire perspective about life and about himself. It makes him wise to his own weaknesses and alert to the strength which is Christ. It doesn't depress him but makes him realistic with himself. So much so that he is never, never *surprised* with his own sins. What, after all, does he expect of a boy living in the Original Sin age? He has the insight of the great priest saint, St. John Vianney. Every day before he began Mass he would look up to the altar and say to Christ, "Be careful, Lord, if you don't watch me, I'll betray You today!" Saint that he was, he was realistic and knew that sin was always a possibility.

We have a classic example of destructive and constructive guilt in the Gospels. Peter and Judas. If you think about it, they both committed the same sin: they both betrayed Christ. Peter said, "I know not the man!" They both felt guilty afterward. They both repented. In fact, Judas went one better and made restitution. He gave back the thirty pieces of silver. But his guilt was of the destructive kind, not like Peter's. Peter wept bitterly but ran to Jesus for forgiveness. Peter's guilt led him out of himself to turn to Jesus as his only hope. Judas, on the other hand, turned to no one. You can almost hear him say what some boys say to themselves, "Oh, I'm no good. I sinned again. I'll never get any better! What's the use? I'll only do it over and over again. Why try? Nobody can help me. Nobody understands me!" That's a pretty big "nobody" when it includes Christ. So Judas, in depression and despair, went and hanged himself.

Constructive guilt is a healthy reaction. Destructive and excessive guilt is indeed bad. But constructive guilt, the feeling of shame of having sinned, the humble and confident turning to Christ as your only hope—this is good. It's the type of guilt that makes saints.

2. CONFESSION

Confession is the place where the guilty Catholic boy normally turns to Christ whether in the private confession of himself and the priest or the "communal" confession of the group. He should probably get a lot more out of this sacrament except that he goes into it with such misunderstandings. One is the notion we mentioned in the chapter on masturbation: the secret attitude of seeking the "instant cure." So many boys confuse going to confession with obtaining the cure, like going to an AA meeting to 'get the cure.' But confession is not an instant cure, it is a *process*. It is a means whereby a boy physically demonstrates (by simply getting up and going to confession) his inner sincerity and holiness in spite of his weaknesses and sins. He must return many times to the confessional because healing, as distinct from that "instant cure" takes time.

Another bad approach to confession is that of shame and embarrassment. Well, we've just seen that a sensible shame is good but it ought not to keep you from confession. We mentioned, again in the chapter on masturbation, that the priest knows the score. He'll not yell but he'll try to help. We recommended that you go back to the same priest all the time so he can learn your habits and your good points and help you better. If you can bring yourself to tell him who you are in the confessional, so much the better. If not, at least indicate you're coming back to him. You're there to contact Jesus, not the priest. And confess precisely. Don't confess adultery (sin with another) if you mean masturbation (sin with self). Don't confess passing fantasy thoughts as "impure thoughts" or seeing something on TV and say you were "looking at impure things" thereby giving the impression that this was deliberate.

Perhaps the biggest obstacle to a good confession in matters of sex is the age-old, highly successful temptation of *hypocrisy*. The adolescent boy is a prime target for this. This is the temptation that says, "Why go to confession. You know you're going to do it all over again. Why be a hypocrite and walk up to receive Communion when the rest of the week you're going to masturbate!" I wonder how many boys stay away from confession for this reason! This temptation is a variation of the "instant cure" error. It's a mass confusion between weakness and sincerity. Because something happens frequently doesn't mean that a person is insincere. A sincere alcoholic who truly wishes he would stop drinking but can't is not a hypocrite. Would you want him to not even try? He can be as weak as they come, but very sincere. He will go to heaven because of his efforts. Do you really think that a boy who has, say, a bad masturbation problem is better off staying away from Christ because he knows "he'll do it again"? Don't you realize that God is the only one in our lives that does not measure us by success but only by effort? If your little brother was lousy in math and didn't even try, you would be annoyed. "At least try!" **you** would yell at him. Then if he tries and got terrible marks, you would be satisfied. You would be satisfied because

you would know that, although he still got the poor
mark, as a person, as a boy, as a human being he grew
better *inside*. He failed as a student of math, but he
passes as a boy of character. So with confession. It is
your symbol of trying, your outward sign of sincerity beneath the weakness. Every confession shouts to God,
"Look, I may be weak. I'm disgusted with this problem. I
know I'm going to do it all over again and you know it
—but I'm here! I'm here to say that failure in one area
doesn't mean failure in all else. I may be failing the subject of "purity" but I intend to pass the subject of "character." I intend to receive Communion tomorrow because
I know that I need Christ's help. Whatever else happens
to me, I want to meet Jesus someday with a good record
of effort, a long list of confessions and communions.
They'll be my pluses to offset my minuses!"

In his book, *Shalom* Father Haring mentions this case:

> I remember a young teenager saying to me, 'Father, ex-
> plain to me how God can be love. How can I believe
> that God loves me when I can't keep myself in the state
> of grace for a single week, even though I pray and really
> want to be good?" Stung by his own inability to over-
> come his difficulties his heart wondered if God was not
> rejecting him, despite his good will. . . . Instead of
> stressing the seriousness of the boy's offense, the confes-
> sor might have emphasized the importance of overcom-
> ing this temporary difficulty. He might have congratu-
> lated the boy on his wonderful display of good will. He
> should say, "So long as you honestly say that you are
> trying, so long as you continue to pray for help to do
> what you can't do yet, then be assured that you are in
> the grace of God. It may be a long, hard battle, but you
> will succeed." One should not be surprised if a penitent

such as this boy begins doubting whether or not he still has good will. . . .⁹

Again, Father Haring is saying what we have tried to say: effort builds both character and sanctity, not success. Frequent confession is a certain and distinguished sign of your effort, a real mark of sincerity. It can and does exist quite well side by side with weakness. The self-charge of hypocrisy is false, a lie, a subtle temptation to get you to throw in the towel. True teenage holiness learns to resist this temptation.

Finally, look upon confession for what it truly is: an act of religion. And, like all genuine acts of religion, the focus is not on yourself but on God—the Father who loved you first before you ever thought of loving Him. The French spiritual writer, Louis Evely has caught this spirit of confession well when he writes:

> Religion consists in those wonders of generosity, love and forgiveness which God does for us. . . . We continually forget that we are not Christians because we love God; we are Christians because we believe that God loves us.

> The prime purpose of confession is not to ensure our moral infallibility. It reveals to us the love and generosity of the Father in forgiving us. . . . If we were not sinners, needing forgiveness even more than bread, we would not know the depth of God's heart. . . . "There shall be more joy in heaven upon one sinner that does penance than upon ninety-nine just who do not need penance"

> We complicate things to such an extent that we forget *the* condition without which all confessions would be farcical: to believe that God loves us. . . .

As we enter the confessional, we say "Bless me, Father, because I have sinned," because I have received this first, this great grace of realizing that I have sinned. We do not say, "Punish me Father; tell me off because I have sinned." But we say, "Father, say a good word to me, encourage me, congratulate me, because God has touched me: I have realized that I am a sinner."

Too often we try to make use of confession itself as a means of doing without God. "Confession doesn't do me any good," one will say, "so I don't go to confession anymore." Or another, "It may do me some good, but not much, because I am always confessing the same faults."

I see what you mean. You would like to use confession as a means of doing without confession. You want to make use of God so that you can do without Him.

But the main purpose of confession is not a means to acquire moral perfection. It is a religious act, it is the occasion of meeting with the Father, a meeting in which you learn how much He loves you, with what joy and tenderness He pardons you, to what lengths His forgiveness will go, and the wonder of it all."[10]

PRACTICAL FOOTNOTE ON CONFESSION

When I was a younger priest I used to think that many teenage boys stayed away from confession because of purity problems. I now know that to be wrong. Their confession going, like their religious life in general, stems from their home example and training. No matter what problems a boy has, if he comes from a home where confession and communion are values, he approaches these sacraments frequently.

However, the purity problem is still a factor and I would like to pass on to you an arrangement I've worked out with the boys in my parish. When they go to confession they have their choice of three approaches. (1) First, is the Regular Confession; that is the boy goes to confession his usual way: telling his sins and getting advice. (2) Next, is the "Bargain" Confession. In this confession the boy simply comes in and says, "Father, I'm here for the Bargain" and this means that he the boy will do all the talking and confessing *but no questions* will be asked by the priest. (3) The third form is the "General" Confession. This is not really an accurate term, but it means that when the boy comes in he says, "Father, I'd like to make a general confession" and in this instance the boy keeps quiet and the *priest* does all the talking. The priest simply runs down quickly the ten commandments and the boys answers "yes" or "no"; if he says "yes" the priest will only ask, "few times or many times" and that's that.

As I've indicated elsewhere, having a regular confessor helps; that is, going back to the same priest. Tell him who you are or, as suggested, use a code name or some indication that you've been to him before.

CHAPTER VII

Discharge or Symbol?

There is, ultimately, only one basic question that every adolescent boy must answer about sex, and how he answers it will define his personality for the rest of his life. The big question is this, "What shall I make of sex: a discharge or symbol?" Another way of phrasing that question is to ask, "What do I intend to *do* with sex? what do I want it to *say* about me?" Such questions are vitally important for the adolescent boy. He is on the way to becoming a man; he's getting a new drive towards sexual activity and he must make up his mind about these questions soon.

Not that any boy's new sexual emotions come suddenly upon him apart from his total personality or apart from the fact that from birth he has been a sexual being. Rather, as the famous doctors about sex, Drs. Masters and Johnson, point out, with adolescence reproductive and glandular sex emerge but only *"as a further dimension of an already existing sexuality."* What do they mean? They mean that a boy is a boy all over, inside and out. "Sexuality" refers to his total state of being boy. He is male in the way he thinks, acts, feels from the top of his head to the bottom of his toes. There is as much "sex" in his fingernail as in his sexual organs. That is, his "maleness" is himself all over. What happens at adolescence is that a boy's sexual drives add a new thrust of sexual emotion to his *already* existing state as a male or a masculine sexual being. His new sexual urges, like all his other emotions of anger, fear, hate, etc., affect him altogether as a person and prepare the whole person for action. It's like driving a car for the first time. The driving is new, but the boy who's driving has been around for a while and is now using his total abilities and emotions in the new thrust of driving. His personality has found a new and exciting means of expression.

So it is with sex. Sex doesn't suddenly emerge. Rather, the new sexual drives simply provide a new and exciting means of expression for the same masculine boy who's been around for thirteen years or so. And, as with his other emotions and strong urges he must decide what he wants to do with them. Shall he merely discharge his new sexual drives whenever he "feels" like it, like he might discharge his anger by hitting his little sister because he "feels" like it? Or, shall he make of sex an expression of himself, his personality, the kind of guy he wants to be? The adolescent boy must come to terms with such questions and try to determine what *meaning* he wants sexual emotion to have in his life. Hence, the title of this chapter: Sex, Discharge or Symbol?

Let's take a look at sex as a discharge. Al is getting real "horney" as the kids say. That is, he's feeling sexy and having a terrific erection. The sexual emotional pressure is there. So is Sue, his girl friend. He starts breathing heavier as he proceeds to touch Sue's breasts and in general makes out with her until he reaches a climax and the seed fluid is released in his pants. It was exciting while it lasted. Now that it's over, what did his sexual activity with Sue really say? Well, it said that Al, like all other boys, is easily excitable in matters of sex. Yes, but what else? It also said that when Al has sexual tension he releases it and uses his girl friend for this purpose (although he would deny "using" her). His act said that he is not too controlled, that he has neither scruples nor hesitation in making sex a discharge. He never even gave it a thought that he might try to discipline or delay his drive. That didn't even enter into his mind. He likes Sue, they're both only in high school and marriage is years off—if at all. There was no commitment here. His sexual activity certainly gave no hint of responsibility. The whole thing was just a discharge. It's hard not to draw the conclusion that Al is rather selfish. But, more important for his future, he is making sex only and merely a discharge in his life. If he continues such behavior with Sue and Mary and Alice and Joan through the years he will have emptied sex of all meaning and made of it only a release-of-pressure affair. If that's what happens sex will never symbolize or "say" anything for Al.

A man named Erikson in his book, *Insight and Responsibility* indicates that adolescents have two choices to make about sex. One is the activity such as I've just described about Al. Or, the other choice is what he calls "disciplined and devoted delay." What a wonderful phrase! Let's look at this alternative of sex and consider sex as symbol rather than merely as discharge.

What is a symbol? A symbol is some outward sign that expresses an inward reality. Giving flowers to a widow, for example, expresses the real but invisible emotion of sympathy. A valentine is an outward symbol of inward fondness. A kiss may be the exterior sign of interior affection. All these things, we say, are symbols. They are not the thing itself, not the reality itself; they're only trying to express it in the most appropriate way. Symbols also extend to other outward signs. For example, the language we use declares something of the inward state of our thoughts and mind. The clothes we wear and the way we wear our hair are outward signs of our invisible posture in life: my long hair, for example, may be a symbol that I'm of the rebellious generation or play in a band. The way my emotions and urges surge to the surface and get expressed are also symbols and tell others what kind of a person I am. My emotional pride of ownership, for example, can lead me to working hard or, unchecked, can lead me to avarice and theft. My emotion of fear can lead me to produce or, unchecked, to cowardice. My emotion of anger can lead me to seeking justice or, unchecked, to murder. Whatever alternatives I choose will say a lot about me. Whatever way I express these emotions tells others the kind of person I am. They are symbols of me, outward signs of my manliness and my general approach to people and things. My sexual emotions and urges are especially revealing about me and very symbolic.

The adolescent boy doesn't often see how symbolic his sexual behavior is and how revealing of the type of person he is. He's apt to feel that he's entitled to "sow his wild oats" sexually and later he'll settle down to chastity. That's fine except it won't work. He will be at 21 what he was at 20. He will be at 20 what he was at 19; he will be at 19 the result of what he's done at 18 and so on. The result of many repeat choices reveals him. We call this character. Easy and frequent sexual activity merely leads him to see sex as a discharge, a habit he's not likely to shake as a married man.

Besides generally symbolizing a boy's approach to life, sex is a symbol in other profound ways too. Of itself it is a deep symbol of total surrender to another and total responsibility. Sexual intercourse in particular is one of the most complete ways that a man and woman can give themselves to each other, a great two-in-one-flesh demonstration of commitment and donation, a great symbol of total love. That word "total" is a key word because it refers to *all* the ways of taking responsibility for another and at *all* times. A husband who is having sexual intercourse with his wife, therefore, is in effect saying this to her:

> Look, I am not just taking you now at this moment. I'm taking you for *all* moments. I am taking your past whatever that has been and I am taking you for the future whatever that may be. I am taking you not only now when you are beautiful and desirable and young and lovely, but I am taking you for twenty years from now even when your hair is gray, your shoulders stooped and your figure heavier. I take you when we quarrel and are angry with each other. I take you when you're sick and aching. I take you when you hurt my feelings, break my heart. I take you even if I should become attracted to a younger and prettier woman or another man's wife. This act of sexual love is not just of the moment for my pleasure (discharge). It is my symbol, my promise to take you—until death!

This is sex as symbol. It is really "saying" something about this husband. It is his generous sign of genuine commitment. The difference between this husband and our friend, Al, is the difference between discharge and symbol. Al's sexual activity is the discharge of a short-

term release. This husband's sexual activity is the symbol
of a long-term commitment.

So, we come back to our original question which we
said must be posed to every adolescent and which he
must answer, "Sex: discharge or symbol for me?" Now
any boy who (wisely) chooses sex as symbol does not of
course, deny that he possesses sexual urges, does not deny
having many and severe temptations to find a quick and
convenient discharge; rather, he simply and freely
chooses that "disciplined and devoted delay" which sym-
bolizes him as a controlled man. He chooses to love another more by withholding of sexual activity than by its
use. Since sex is such a high symbol he decides never to
use it casually but to save it until it means what it says.
He chooses to love another more by his "devoted delay"
than by impulsive discharge.

At the risk of belaboring the point, let me put it another way and give other examples to show how other
symbols can be and are used or withheld as "devoted
delay." We'll start with this diagram:

flowers	g	
kiss	u	
handshake	i	The Loved
candy	d	One
sex	e	

On the left side is a random list of the ways I can symbolize affection. On the right side is The Loved One, the one I
want to show affection and concern to. In the middle is
the guide to determine in each case whether I use the
symbols or not use them as a part of my "disciplined and
devoted delay." Let's take the flowers. Suppose that I'm
on my way to see my girl friend. I've got a little money in

my pocket so as I pass the flower shop I drop in and spend five dollars on a nice bouquet; I get to my girl friend's house, ring the bell. When she opens the door and notices that I'm hiding something behind my back she asks, "What do you have there for me?" I reply that I'm not going to tell her. After kidding around a while I finally bring out the flowers. She's thrilled and gives me a big kiss. Now six months later I go through the same routine: money, flowers, ringing the door bell. This time, however, when I bring the flowers forth she exclaims, "Oh, no! Take them away! This is my hay fever season and I'll sneeze my head off!" At that I pause, look at my flowers in my hand, think of what they cost me and reply, "Look, girl, if you think I'm going to waste five bucks. . . ." and I shove the flowers smack into her face!

While we're mentally chuckling over this scene we should take another look at our diagram. Flowers are listed as one way to express love. The Loved One is listed as my guide on the use or non-use of flowers. It so happens that at one time I can express love by giving the flowers and another time I can express love by *withholding* the flowers. The Loved One in both instances is indeed my guide because what is best for her should rule the day. I was, however, frustrated and I merely discharged that frustration by shoving the flowers into her face. The flowers, meant to be the symbol of love, now turn into an uncontrolled release of my annoyance. Result: I made of my emotion a discharge instead of a symbol.

Take the candy listed as a symbol of showing love. If at one time I give my girl a box of candy as a symbol of my love I may well withhold or delay it out of love if it is discovered that she has sugar in her blood. For me to get angry and start shoving candy down her throat regardless is to reflect on the genuineness of my love. Surely my devoted delay would be a far better sign of affection than the simple discharge of my frustration in stuffing her with candy.

Sex is also listed as a symbol of love. True. And I would like to show my love through sexual activity. I know, of course, that sex, like the flowers and the candy, etc. is not love itself; it's only one way to show love. When should I use it? Well, the same rule applies to sex as to the flowers or candy or any other symbol: when it's good for the Loved One. That's the guide. If it's not really good for the Loved One, then my sexual activity, no matter what I say or what sweet words I use with her, is essentially only a discharge of sexual tension. If it's good for her, then my sexual activity is truly symbolic of my love just as the flowers and the candy at the right time are genuine symbols of love.

Well, that leaves us with one final question: Is sexual activity with a girl good *for her* before marriage? Does it show genuine love? or do I love her more by the disciplined and devoted delay of sex? To answer this, we've got to get even more involved in this chapter with a difficult concept: what is love?

We might as well start by saying what love is *not*, namely, feeling. Every boy and girl knows that feelings and emotions certainly enter into love, but they are not love itself. The simple reason is that feelings are so fickle and love has to be more substantial than feeling good one day and hateful the next. In fact, true love and opposite feelings can coexist as when a mother spanks her child in anger or you have one of those fights with your father. The emotions and feelings can range anywhere from hate to anger and yet there's no doubt, not even for an instant, that love is there.

Anyway, we can define love as "the will and effort to forget oneself and to do what is best for another." This definition contains one of the best rule-of-thumb guides for detecting the beginnings of a mature love: when you really begin to think more of another than of yourself, really begin to *care* more about another than yourself, love is starting to grow in you. Now in the examples we gave we discovered that "what's best for another" is a valid guide and our use of the flowers or the candy had to follow this guide. Here, of course, our question is about sex and if pre-marriage sex is good for a girl. There are several reasons, I think, why it is not and, therefore, why a boy's approach to sex with a girl must take the rule of "disciplined and devoted delay" rather than a discharge.

First of all, there is the danger of pregnancy outside of marriage and therefore outside of commitment. A boy might answer that these days she can be "protected" by taking the pill or some other contraceptive. But no contraceptive is foolproof. Outside of an operation chastity is the only perfect guarantee against pregnancy. Dear Abby puts it in her inimitable way when she remarks that the only perfect oral contraceptive is the word "no."

But, for the sake of argument, let's say that pregnancy is not a danger. Is the girl better off as a person and is she better respected as a person for having sexual intercourse before marriage? Can any boy and girl be so casual about sex outside of marriage and then easily make it so meaningful and committed in marriage? Aren't they both establishing a pattern of weakness which will follow them into marriage? As Dr. Duvall says in her book, *Why Wait Till Marriage?:*

> But wait, you say. "Sure I'll settle down when the time comes, but right now it's only natural that I get some release." You may just do that. But, remember that the overwhelming tendency is to continue doing what you have done before.

> The chances are that you speak much as you have been doing through the years. You can tell a man from New England from a fellow from the deep South, as soon as you hear him talk. Why? Because each man tends to speak as he learned to talk when he was growing up. Is there any reason to believe that the same thing does not happen in sexual expression? If a fellow always has played fast and loose with girls, is he sure to drop all these habits once he gets married? Will he no longer be attracted to other women? If he is, will he not want to do as he always has before, and make a play for them? What assurance have you that the marriage ceremony will change the kind of thing you always have done?

> The only thing you can be fairly sure about is that you will probably be very much the same person after you marry that you have been before. Getting married is a big step, but it cannot change human nature. You need not kid yourself when you marry, either you or your mate will all of a sudden be something neither of you has been before. You cannot hope to reform your partner or yourself. You both may become more mature. You may settle down, at least for a while. But you will always be the kind of personalities you brought to your marriage in the first place.[11]

Is easy sex really good for a wife and mother to be?

How about the boy: is this good practice for being a husband and father? What about trust? You say, what about it? Well, if a boy and girl can in principle have sexual relations outside of marriage why cannot this same principle operate when they are married? Trust gets a hard going over by boys and girls who are impure before marriage. You may not think so now, but just pause for a moment: would you blame the husband of a formerly unchaste girl for being suspicious about her when she's away for a month somewhere visiting? Does the wife of a formerly uncontrolled boy friend really think he's being chaste and true when he's away at that convention in Chicago for three months? And if either ever discovers infidelity about each other, why are they so terribly, terribly upset? Yet they are! And all the while, as unmarried boys and girls having intercourse, they were making such infidelity possible and probable.

Sex before marriage hurts a girl because it exploits her and leaves her never quite sure whether she's got a commitment from this guy or is likely to be turned in for another model. She's never quite sure whether he's "using" her or not. Without the commitment of marriage she's always susceptible to rejection. Sex without symbolizing total responsibility for her understandably leaves her uneasy. As Dr. Seymour Haleck points out in his article, "Sex and Mental Health on Campus" (italics mine):

> ... If a girl accepts the new attitudes and wishes to have sexual relations with a boy on the basis of mutual affection and love, she must still define the strength of their commitment. Inevitably she must struggle with the question of *how close two people can be when not bound to one another by the responsibilities of a marital contract.*

Any relationship out of wedlock is plagued with certain ambiguities. The girl must struggle with questions such as: "Will the first argument or sign of incompatibility lead to a dissolution of the relationship and search for a new partner?" If this does happen, will she simply deceive herself into promiscuity under the rationalization that each new relationship is meaningful? Will she "kid herself" into believing that she is in love when in actuality she is only succumbing to social and sexual pressures? It is my belief that these ambiguities have been heightened by changes in attitudes towards sex. The stresses associated with choosing or sustaining sexual relationships before marriage *have had an especially intense effect upon female students.* For some students such stresses have been critical factors in precipitating severe emotional disorders. . . .[12]

Dr. Mary S. Calderone of the Sex Information and Education Council of the U.. S., in a talk to Vassar freshmen said:

There is absolutely no possibility of having sexual relationship without irrevocably meshing a portion of your two non-physical selves. Sex is each time such a definitive experience that a part of each of you remains forever a part of the other. How many times and how casually are you willing to invest a portion of your total self and to be the custodian of a like investment from the other person without the sureness of knowing that these investments are being made for keeps?

Dr. Duvall says this:

The ability truly to love and be loved is learned through the years. Too early focus of love feelings in sexual intercourse cuts off the ability to love deeply and broadly as human beings can. It is so that they may learn to love

> that a couple postpones complete intimacy until they are
> ready—as persons, and as a pair.[13]

Again, Dr. Duvall says:

> Of course you will love the one you marry. The one
> thing that will make this married love unique through
> the years is that it alone is expressed sexually. Saving
> sex for marriage gives you something very special to
> share with one another, which no one else can have.
> Into your married love, then, you can pour all your feel-
> ings as husband and wife, co-partners in building a mar-
> riage and family together.[14]

You see what a boy asks a girl to do if he wants sex
before commitment. He's hurting her future and her
growth as a person and this is not real love. Dear Abby
as usual puts the whole case simply when she says in her
book, *Dear Teen-Ager:*

> Dear Abby, Should I prove my love?
> Girls need to "prove their love" through illicit sex re-
> lations like a moose needs a hatrack.
> Why not "prove your love" by sticking your head in
> the oven and turning on the gas? Or by playing leap-frog
> out in the traffic? It's about as safe.
> Clear the cobwebs out of your head. Any fellow who
> asks you to "prove your love" is trying to take you for
> the biggest, most gullible fool who ever walked. That
> proving bit is one of the oldest and rottenest lines ever
> invented!
> Does *he* love *you?* It doesn't sound like it. Someone
> who loves you wants what is best for you. But now
> figure it out: he wants you to—
> > commit an immoral act
> > surrender your virtue
> > throw away your self-respect

risk the loss of your precious reputation
and risk getting into trouble.

Does that sound as though he wants what's best for
you? This is the laugh of the century: he wants what's
best for *him*. . . . he wants a thrill he can brag about at
your expense.

Love? Who's kidding whom? A boy who loves a girl
would sooner cut off his right arm than hurt her. If you
want my opinion, this self-serving so-and-so has already
proved that he *doesn't* love you. . . .[15]

Another point is that sex outside of marriage isolates
the sexual act from the total package of living together.
Where's the symbol of sex's total responsibility if a boy
and girl do that? Sex, as we have seen, is supposed to
symbolize total commitment and here a couple is isolating it from total living together. There's no bills, sickness,
hospitalization, mortgage, children, hardship, etc. To iso-
late sex from all this total livingness is both unreal and
unnatural. To do so would really be seeking and stealing
the secondary joys of sex apart from responsibility. Such
a declaration of irresponsibility before marriage doesn't
argue too well for what will happen after marriage.

Finally, for the believer in God there is the question of
sin. Sin not because sex is involved, but because irresponsibility and deep uncharity are.

Such are some of the reasons why I believe that sexual
activity with a girl outside of marriage is not real love.
Sex before marriage is not good for her and, as we have
seen, what is good for her must be my guide whether it's
a question of the flowers, the candy or sex. Others have
written much more in detail and much more persuasively
about such matters. I would strongly recommend these

books. *Love, Sex and the Person* by Peter Bertocci. It's published by Sheed and Ward and is good for older boys and college boys. Dr. Duvall's book *Why Wait Till Marriage?* we've already mentioned. The best book, in my opinion, for today's teenager is Father Joseph Champlin's paperback with the intriguing title *Don't You Really Love Me?* (Ave Maria Press).

Anyway, we come back to the ultimate answer as to why there should be no deliberate sex before marriage and that answer is love. Any girl (whether she knows it or not) deserves the comfort, stability and protection of a permanent relationship. To give her less than that is to dishonor and exploit her. Worse, it is a christian failure to love. Therefore, in the case of any boy the greatest act of love, both for himself and for the girl, is his free decision to exercise that "disciplined and devoted delay" of which we spoke before. Once more, then, when it comes to the ultimate question: "Sex: discharge or symbol?" he must choose sex as a symbol—the symbol of himself, the symbol of his total and permanent donation to another in love, a fitting symbol, disciplined and delayed, for the commitment of marriage.

CHAPTER VIII

The Dating Game

"After years of examination and comparison, I have come to the conclusion that an important contributing factor in this deterioration of American marriage is our unique and nationwide custom of dating. . . . When dating invades the junior high school, as it did long ago, and even the elementary school, as it is now doing, it may be a negative and dangerous thing. . . ."[16] This statement about dating is from Doctor David R. Mace, former executive director of the American Association of Marriage Counselors. Let me add one more quote. It's from *Life* magazine which several years ago ran a series of articles on marriage. In that series the author had this to say:

> The early age at which boys and girls start falling in love nowadays has been the subject of much recent discussion, pro and con. Apparently the facts are even more startling than most writers have realized. One of the newest studies, made in a prosperous and pleasant Georgia town, showed that nine out of 10 of the fifth graders —10 years old—claimed to have "sweethearts." Nearly half the boys and more than a third of the girls had had experience with kissing, a fact which led one of the authors, Dr. Carlfred B. Broderick, to wonder, "if they're kissing at 10, what do you expect they'll be doing at 15?" Why dating should have replaced dolls and baseball gloves is one of the mysteries of our time. . . .[17]

These two quotations indicate that somebody's playing

games with dating and the consequences are very serious. Somebody's forgetting to ask the essential questions about dating which are, "What is dating for, anyway?" and "Why is too early dating a negative and dangerous thing?" Let's try to answer these questions in this chapter.

Dating is to develop good and honest human relationships between the sexes. Dating teaches you and a girl to know and understand each other. For those who eventually decide on marriage as their career, dating is very important as a preparation. Dating is also discovery time. A boy and girl learn a lot about what each one holds in value. They can discover what each thinks about school, sports, art, music, the war, family life and religion.

Dating should normally become an interest at puberty, that is, when those sex gland chemicals go to the brain and make a boy and girl interested in sex and interested in each other. We described this in the first chapter of the book. I say "normally" the interest begins at puberty, but *abnormally,* as Dr. Mace and *Life* magazine point out, dating has gone down to the kids who have no chemical reaction as yet. Such kids go on dates, not because of the attraction resulting from a sex drive, but because it's the "in" thing to do. Dating is like smoking used to be. Once only the college kids smoked. Then it went down to the high school kids. Now, as you know, many of the kids in grammar school smoke. It makes them feel grown up and "big." They're "doing their thing." Substitute "dating" for "smoke" and you've got the picture.

We quoted *Life* as saying, "Why dating should have replaced dolls and baseball gloves is one of the mysteries of our time." Well, I don't think it's *that* much of a mystery. I think that dating has become a game kids play be-

cause society and the merchandisers and some parents
have forced it on them. A lot of people are happy if underage kids date. Mommy and Daddy are apt to feel
proud of a eighth grade girl who can be attractive enough
to catch a high school junior. The merchants are happy if
she dates early because then she will need more new
wardrobes and dresses and make-up and hair color and
all the other accessories to match. "Society" would include one or two popular kids who start early dating and
put the pressure on the others. How many kids you know
of started dating in grammar school? Yet, Dr. Mace and
others who ought to know, take a dim view of too early
dating as a preparation for marriage. Why? Let's look at
a few answers—answers which may help you to determine your approach to dating in general.

First, too early dating throws together boys and girls
who may not be emotionally ready to profit from the experience. They are simply not yet capable of developing
those good and honest relationships which are the purpose of dating. There's a certain "readiness," doctors tell
us, for certain things of life. There is, for instance, a
"walking" readiness. This means that when your little sister is ready to walk, she'll walk, not before that. When
her muscles and coordination are ready, she'll walk.
There's a "reading" readiness teachers tell us. When the
eye and brain reach a certain level and have sufficient
coordination good reading will occur. Before that, to
force the walking or the reading is a waste of time. So,
too, there's a human relationship readiness. To force this
kind of readiness beforehand is a waste of time and also
even harmful.

To put it another way, to start dating too early places a

boy or girl on the first step on the staircase of successful human relationships before they can actually climb those steps. Let me illustrate what we might call "The Successful Staircase of Human Relationships" in the following diagram and explain what I mean.

5. Total Commitment, sealed by sexual intercourse, The Great Symbol

4. Partial Commitment: going steady, courtship

3. Communication, discovering compatibility

2. Friendship, companionship

1. Physical, sexual attraction

The first step on the staircase of successful human relationships is attraction. This attraction occurs, as we just reminded you, as a result of the chemical changes of the body. Such a chemical process is quite necessary if boys and girls—natural preadolescent enemies—are ever to get together. This physical and sexual attraction will induce boys and girls to mix cautiously together in groups. This group interaction is very good and gives them the opportunity of experimentation in getting along with each other. This group interaction also provides them with the opportunity to develop the next step.

This second step is the beginning of genuine and life-long friendships and companionships, both with the opposite and the same sex. This step of building friendships with buddies and others is very vital and is not something

that is done overnight. It requires lots of time and has to
go through a lot of ups and downs to become a strong
bond. Many years, in fact, are really needed to test and
firm up true friendships. Many years are needed also to
provide for a change in taste as boys and girls mature
throughout the years. The guy you were so friendly with
in the seventh grade may not be your closest friend now.
You don't dislike each other, but you've "outgrown" each
other. A boy some girl once considered a "living dream"
she now considers a "nightmare." "How could I ever
have liked *him?*" I've heard more than one girl exclaim.
Well, she really did like him once, but she's older now.
Her tastes have changed in boys just as they have
changed in clothes and the shades of lipstick. This second
step of building friendships is most essential and it definitely needs time. The capacity for friendship needs room
to grow and develop. You can't hurry it.

The third step on our staircase is communication. This
means not only just talking with another, but revealing
and learning. You reveal your secret self to another, your
fears, aspirations, wishes, thoughts. But you also learn
how to *listen.* You try to see that a girl is so different and
interprets life in a way that you, as a boy, do not. Remember what we said about love in the last chapter? We
defined it as the will and effort to forget oneself in the interest of doing what's best for another. In this step of real
communication this "forgetting" begins to take place.
Your whole attention is on another; your whole desire to
understand her. Good communication over the years with
many, many boys and girls will eventually lead you to
especially good communication with one particular girl.
By your increased ability to dialogue, to both reveal

yourself and learn of her, you will determine that you and this girl are "compatible." That word, like so many of its Latin counterparts we've seen in this book, is so revealing. It means literally to "suffer or endure together." When a boy and a girl discover through good communication, that they can endure the joys and sorrows of life together, they are said to be "compatible." This discovery will lead to step four, the partial commitment of going steady or courtship.

In this fourth step, friendship and communication deepen. Now they revolve around what will affect the couple most deeply and most intimately. How does each feel about marriage, about children, family life, money, in-laws, God? What does each think about sex and does each view sex as the great symbol of their total commitment and togetherness? Where will they live? Can they afford to get married? And so on. When this deep exchange is complete they decide on the final step of marriage. In this last and final step they go before the Church (the priest) and the State (the best man and maid of honor) and publicly declare their acceptance of mutual responsibility. With that public declaration of responsibility they receive from God, of course, the right to all of the full and secondary joys of sex (see chapter 3). Pledging the hardship they are now entitled to the reward.

Such is the normal progress of dating and what we've just described is a good mental outline for any boy to keep in mind when he dates. Not that he has to be so determined and calculating about it, but in his dating experiences he should have floating in the back of his mind the real purposes of dating and that there are certain essential steps to be developed, and a certain pacing is necessary to make dating an experience and not a game.

Dating is a game when the steps are not taken one at a time and with care. What happens (which provoke the remarks of Dr. Mace) is that some kids arrive at step one and then jump right into step four, the going steady plateau. They do not carefully respond to the many in friendship and communication, but get into a rut with the one. They do not expand their personalities but put all their emotional eggs into one basket. They do not mature in friendship and hardly make any progress in communication which requires a great deal of time and many people and so they stumble into marriage. Why marriage? Well, what else do you do for an encore if you've been going steady since the seventh grade? In a few years such people will be divorced. Nine times out of ten the reason given for the divorce will be more accurate than they ever realize: incompatibility. How true! They could not endure the joys and sorrows of life together because they did not have enough preparation.

I have met, in the course of many years of marriage counseling, many couples who raced through and skipped over the steps of the staircase of human relationships. Not only did they not love each other any more, they didn't even *like* each other! They aren't friends much less spouses. They can't communicate. Sometimes I have closed my eyes listening to some thirty-five-year-old wife and have said to myself, "Good Lord, she's a thirteen-year-old!" I meant that while her age is thirty-five, her emotional capacity is that of a little girl. Apparently her capacity for good friendships and good communications were never developed. That's why our Dr. Mace feels that early dating is an important factor contributing to the deterioration of American marriage.

I must briefly mention one more point. I have taught seniors in high school for many years and I know that many, in fact most, of the kids do not have a regular dating life. At least in the sense of steady dating and very frequent dating with one girl. I have discovered that the kids talk an awfully good game, but in little private surveys and questionnaires the average high school student does not emerge the hot and heavy dater he would have you to believe. I mention this to support the kids—and maybe you're one of them—who really don't want to date and feel odd if they don't. Even at the White House Conference of Youth a few years ago the teenagers kept bringing up this fact that many of them were not really interested in a lively dating life although they admitted that they were pressured about this not only by some of the other kids but by teachers and even their parents as well.

We can sum up our advice on dating by telling the reader that dating is healthy and normal and has a purpose. This purpose is learning to get along. There are certain steps to successful getting along and to rush and race through these steps is unwise and short-sighted. Too early dating by immature people can actually be harmful. Happy marriages are built on careful dating patterns. When a boy dates—which he may reasonably choose not to do until he's out of school—he must have in mind that there's seriousness behind the fun and purpose behind the experience.

No chapter on dating is complete without the inevitable questions about kissing and petting and making out on a date. Well, we've really answered those questions in the last chapter when we spoke of the definition of love:

doing what is best for another. Passionate or French kissing, petting and making out are not really best for the girl who hopes to be a faithful wife and earnest mother and the boy who wishes to be a loyal husband and chaste father. Does that mean that nothing goes on a date? No, not necessarily. Signs of affection may be shown. The respectful kiss, the touch, the gentle embrace are allowable. So are any primary sexual joys that come from a boy's respectful encounter with his girl. The serious boy who wishes to honor his girl and not exploit her learns his degree of tolerance. He learns where he must draw the line. In addition he also takes into account the demonstrated power of the Law of Progression.

The Law of Progression is Original Sin at work. This law says that a larger dosage of anything is needed to achieve the same kicks which beget greater kicks. In plain English this means that the more you get (sexually) the more you want. Most teenagers are rather naive on this point when they are cautioned about the Law of Progression. In fact, they're insulted and consider any adult who gives them such warning as having a dirty mind. They protest their goodness and sincerity and ask, "Don't you trust me?" What they don't realize is that their goodness and sincerity are not being called into question. The issue at stake is the Law of Progression, that urging sprung from Original Sin that pushes a couple further than they really want to *regardless* of their sincerity and goodness. Any warnings from adults on dating are simply prudent observations of human nature and not a lack of trust. Let me share a not uncommon situation with you to shed further light on what we're talking about here.

Here is the scene in my rectory office. Sitting on a chair is a girl all of sixteen and all pregnant. Her father and mother are there. No one else. I ask her how long she's known the boy who got her pregnant and she replies that she's been going out with him for three years. I'm not the world's greatest math brain but even I can figure simple arithmetic: "Let's see now. That would make you only thirteen when you started going with this boy. You mean to say that your parents allowed you to go out on single and steady dating with a boy at thirteen?" Here the mother, wanting to justify her permission or at least tolerance, chimes in and says, "Oh, Father, but they were such good kids!" I must confess that this leaves me totally unimpressed. I, in the immortal words of Mae West, merely reply, "Goodness has nothing to do with it!"

How naive of those parents not to remember the Law of Progression. If such parents rightfully tell me of their children's goodness they should equally inform me that these same good children nevertheless have Original Sin with all its built-in weaknesses which will show themselves in the working out of the Law of Progression. Yet, for some reason, parents refuse to admit not only that their sons and daughters have Original Sin but that they even possess sexual organs and sexual drives at all! In fact, most Catholic parents are heretics! You know why? Because our Catholic Church teaches that only one person was ever born without Original Sin and that was Mary with her privilege of the Immaculate Conception, yet these parents all think that their children got in on the same privilege. Again, not only do most parents think that their Johnny or Mary have no sexual organs or sexual drives, but they firmly believe that these children exist

in the state that Adam had before the Fall. That girl in
my office I was mentioning above, I really believe that
her getting pregnant had nothing to do with her or her
boy friend being bad. I believe, however, that her getting
pregnant had everything to do with them both being born
in Original Sin. They simply could not go together for
three years and still be content only to hold hands. They
finally buckled under to the Law of Progression. Indeed,
going beyond what you really want to do is a constant
and proven reality. If you still don't believe me, ask your-
selves these three questions: (1) Have you ever masturbated and really didn't want to? (2) How many kids in
your high school got married while in school or shortly
after and how many were pregnant? and (3) Have you
ever known or heard of any unwed mothers? The answers
to these questions are genuine proof of the existence of
the pull-to-evil which we call Original Sin and that the
Law of Progression really operates.

But we're concerned with the average boy. Being
human and with the best intention to hold fast to his
promised "disciplined and devoted delay" of sexual activity, he may not always succeed. Passion is strong and self
mastery is hard and he might go, on occasion, further
with a girl than he really intends. Knowing that he must
be different from the crowd, refusing to be pulled in to
the "everybody's doing it" routine, he tries harder at self
control the next time. He prays and asks God's help. And
he finds it a lot easier if he's practicing self-control for the
right reason. Not because he thinks sin is connected with
sex, but rather because he loves too much to use it without responsibility. In confession his words should be,

"Father, I confess that I didn't love my girl enough!" Controlling one's dating relationships by love of the girl rather than by fear of the sin will help the relationship to grow.

Added to his efforts must be common sense. God never excuses a human being from that and does not go around dropping personal miracles to offset the normal course of nature. By this I mean that a boy must have certain respectful preliminaries worked out before he goes on a date. He should have a determined place to go, not just "going out" and riding around. He'll soon park if that's the case and that will lead to trouble. Secondly, he should double date for there's safety in numbers. If he and his girl are friendly and honest (and religious) enough, they can tell each other their difficulties and the girl can learn the signals of his sexual stress and guide him. Otherwise, if he does spend all night parking he cannot expect God to suspend his nerve endings and not permit him to get aroused. It's like dieting for weeks, gazing at a chocolate nut sundae and praying, "Oh God, please don't let me eat it!" All that I can say is that a boy is pushing God awfully close to the brink of a miracle if he wants that prayer answered. So too with putting oneself in a situation where it would be almost impossible not to respond to overpowering stimulation. Such sexual brinkmanship is flirting too much with human nature and that's why common sense is the other part of a boy's prayer life in dating.

I want to close this chapter with a short paper I wrote for girls a few years ago. A good girl is perhaps the greatest help to a boy on a date. This paper was written to encourage her to be that help. Here is what it says:

A GOOD GIRL.......
is one who helps her date to be pure. In fact, there is
seldom a more effective motive for a boy to be pure than
a girl whom he admires and respects.

Consider this example. Let's say that every boy is a born
alcoholic. Every time they go out on a date the boy asks
the girl for a drink of scotch which he knows she has in
her purse. He will use the age-old line of course: "If you
love me" he will say, "you'll give me a drink." If the girl
is not sure of herself (and doesn't know the real meaning of the word 'love') she will hesitate but give him the
drink.

A drink or two every date. That's the way it goes. Finally she marries him and now declares that he is an alcoholic and wants him to stop drinking.

He replies that now he's reached the point where he
can't. He's hooked. He's lost all control; and besides it's
a fine time for her to call a stop now. Why didn't she
stop him when he first started? She was the one who ca-
tered to his weakness and brought him to this stage; and,
anyway, if she won't give him a drink he'll go somewhere else where he can get one.

So it is with sex. Even the best boy in the whole world
has a very strong God-given urge to sex—much, much
stronger than a girl's (there are excellent reasons for this
which we can't go into now). Even the best boy has a
built-in weakness in this regard. He will try to get what
he can from a girl sexually and if she gives in to him he
is pleased—but not in his heart. Because although he
enjoys the momentary pleasure he worries about the
long-range trouble he's headed for. He knows that sex,

like food and drink and temper, must be controlled and that as a human being he can and ought to control it; he detests his increasing need and eventually loses respect for the girl he really wanted to say No.

And naturally as he plays with sex often enough he becomes a sexual alcoholic and when they marry she must shed many and many a tear over a husband who cannot control himself (especially during those weeks and months they must be apart for physical reasons) or who becomes unfaithful.

(Later on, when she is consulting the Marriage Counsellor who asks her why in the world she started him on drink knowing his weakness, she will say, "But, Doctor, I loved him!"—Not unlike the girl who today says in response to the priest's warning in the confessional that she stop going steady with the boy if there is sin and no justification, "But, Father, I love him!")

Love is made of stern stuff. It's the ability to do what's best for the beloved, even to the point of strictness and sacrifice. Like the mother who refuses the shiny razor blade to the infant. Like the father who sets guidelines to too late hours. Like the girl who says "No!" to her boy friend.

By no stretch of the imagination could a girl think that a mere marriage ceremony is going to change a boy overnight. He (and indeed she) will be *exactly* the same after the wedding as before. They will both get out of the marriage what they bring to it. If they bring a series of weaknesses, sins and impurities then the marriage has already failed: unhappiness and perhaps divorce are just around the corner.

A good girl is a great help to a boy. *She trains him.* She helps him to be pure because she has enough sense to know that, according to the laws of nature, a pure boy is a pure man, a pure date is a pure husband, a pure boy friend is a faithful spouse.

She helps him to save himself as she saves herself so that they do not give themselves away over the years bit by bit so that they have nothing left for marriage, but they save themselves for the full, spontaneous and happy life of love together forever.

(Perceptive boys will note as they grow older that a girl who is interested enough and loves them enough to help them in their fight for chastity will make the ideal wife: one who always tries to bring about the best in her husband).

A girl is like the Tabernacle with only one key. That key she saves for her husband who alone can open the door and have holy communion with her through all of their marriage, for now—and into eternity.

CHAPTER IX

Virginity and Marriage

"Hugh Hefner is a virgin!" This is one of those wall scribblings called graffiti one frequently sees. The joke is, of course, that Hugh Hefner the publisher of *Playboy* and keeper of all those bunnies should be a virgin—one who has not had sexual intercourse. As the old comedian Bert Lahr used to say, "It is to laugh!" I think the humor, however, extends far beyond Mr. Hefner's virginity. I think that often the humor is just about virginity itself. I mean, suppose someone called you a virgin? Would you like that? It's like what the jazzy writer, Tom Wolfe, says about girls. He says, imagine calling a girl "wholesome!" What girl in her right mind would want that said about her? It's practically the same thing as saying that she's square and cold and dull and proper. The word conjures up a prim girl with glasses, her hair in a bun and a flat chest. "Wholesome!" the nerve! Any girl wants the world to know that she's got as much sexiness as the next one and is ready to play sex games with anyone who's willing. Don't call her wholesome! Yick!

The average boy reacts the same way. He doesn't want anybody even thinking he's a virgin. Why he should feel this way is not too hard to understand. Like the word "wholesome" the word "virgin" carries with it the connotation of being unmasculine. A boy who is a virgin (it is thought) has no sex drive to speak of or is not interested in girls (maybe he's queer?). Being a virgin sounds so stupid and is a reflection on one's manhood, whatever that is. It's like saying that a boy can't even get a good erection. He doesn't have what it takes to "lay" a girl.

Proving that one "has what it takes" to be a man by having sexual intercourse is proving nothing at all. There are those who have had sexual intercourse who have shown themselves to be fearful, greedy, cowardly and traitorous. The presence or absence of sexual experience has nothing to do with one's manliness. Wasn't it Peter, the married man, who denied Christ? Wasn't it John, the teenage virgin, who stayed beneath the cross when everyone else ran away?

We've got to get some sense into what virginity means. In spite of a bad press, being a virgin needs no apology any more than being a married non-virgin does. It's simply a kind of a life that is freely chosen. Nothing in scripture or tradition says that Jesus ever apologized for being a virgin. The one thing we do know about Him was that He gave Himself to others, served others and put His life right on the line as He, with His strong, manly body, underwent the scourging, the nail-driving and the hanging on the cross.

What is virginity? A basic, negative definition is that virginity is the absence of sexual intercourse. But virginity means more than that or should mean more than that. Virginity is not negative, but positive. Virginity is the absence of sexual intercourse or the absence of the "one-to-one" commitment *in order that a person may give himself to a wider commitment*. The virgin, ideally, is the person who scatters his donated love over a wider area than marriage. He (or she) lives for service to the community. Freed of the immediate obligations of a wife and children he is open to others in service. This "openness to service" is the essence of virginity. As we said, Jesus was a virgin. So was St. Paul. Peter was not a virgin nor are your father or mother. Each has his own calling. Each serves his own way. There should be no special downgrading of either vocation.

Both the virgin and the married man may be in their vocations for the wrong reasons. The married man may be married simply because "it's the thing to do" without any real commitment and any real surrender of himself to his wife and to his domestic life. Or he feels that he needs someone to look after him and cook his meals. Or he's afraid of living alone in the world. Or he's acknowledged St. Paul's advice and feels that it's better to marry and place his sexual urges in the right place than to burn with lust outside of marriage.

The virgin may be a virgin because he's afraid of sex. He or she is frigid. He may think that sex is "dirty." He may be ashamed even of the primary joys of sex. He may be selfish and not really be able to share with another in love. He may be a virgin just by default: he never got around to marrying. He may have become a dedicated virgin (such as a brother or a priest) without realizing its full meaning and now wants to undo that dedication and marry so that another human being can unleash his love potential and make him a better man (such, for example, might be the priest or religious who asks for permission to marry).

But, like the married man, the virgin may be in his vocation for the right reasons. He may feel a sense of commitment and, as a single man, join Vista or Project Head Start or the Peace Corps or the religious life or just

quietly serve where needed. He's there to give of himself
to the community without hindrance. He can be free to
move around and serve the community where he can do
the most good. He can be "married" to the community as
it were. The priest is such a man. He is officially married
to the community. The priest is a boy who grew up and
decided to give to the many with the freedom that only
virginity gives. As a boy, of course, he is a sexual being.
He knows and enjoys all of the primary joys of sex yet.
(As one priest said to a boy who noticed him looking at a
pretty girl going by, "Well, Joe, just because I'm on a diet
doesn't mean that I can't look at the menu!") As for his
sexual drives and his normal and natural desires for the
secondary and deliberate pleasures of sex, he reroutes
them into his service to the community.

The priest feels like St. Paul who said:

> An unmarried man can devote himself to the Lord's af-
> fairs, all he need worry about is pleasing the Lord; but a
> married man has to bother about the world's affairs and
> devote himself to pleasing his wife; he is torn two ways
> (1 Cor 7:32).

This doesn't mean, of course, that married people have
no time to give to God or can't become holy. St. Paul
means, that, *everything else being equal,* virginity provides the way of freeing a person so that he can devote
himself entirely to God's people. Because no one woman
has a claim on his heart, he can more readily give it to
all. The priest is not a life-time gift to one person; he is
the gift of himself to whoever needs him. His virginity is
his freedom to move on where others need his care and
help. No one person having a claim on him means that
everybody has a claim on him.

The new Dutch catechism puts it this way:

> The unmarried state is not a state without love. On the
> contrary, the only motive for its existence is love. And it
> is not an existence without a body. The man cherishes
> no woman and begets no child. The woman embraces
> no man and bears no child. But the body after all is
> there for many other things besides sexual intercourse.
> It is there to be kind, to utter the truth, to be a sign in a
> thousand ways of all that man can be, to be the starting
> point of service of many and thus to be fruitful. . . .
>
> But it remains true, it will be said, that they do not get
> married. The growth of the seed, the waiting womb, the
> heart to be given to another—all is in vain. No—it is
> not in vain, but simply a subordinate part in the totality
> of being a fully-grown man or woman. Religious re-
> nounce marriage but not the development of their
> human personality. A nursing sister, a teaching sister,
> does her life's work as a woman. A missionary does the
> work of a man. Physical sex is not exercised, but it must
> of course be there to make someone a real man or
> woman, so that they can have the real goodness of an
> adult person. In this sense no faculty of body or heart is
> superfluous. We understand that Christ was fully a man.
> It was as a man that he brought the good news to man-
> kind.
>
> Those who are unmarried for the sake of the kingdom
> try to be fully prepared, through prayer and work, and
> so to be fruitful in ways for which others are often not
> free. Their heart is given in many ways to different men,
> through whom and in whom they find the one, the con-
> stant, and the true. This shows how essential faith is in
> the religious life. For how could anyone choose to love
> many, without giving his heart to One?[18]

A married man is capable of committing adultery. He does this if he takes his exclusive symbol of sex, pledged only to his wife, and tries to share it with another. His own selfish pleasure seeking led him to overrule his symbolic commitment to his wife. The dedicated virgin can commit adultery too. Not necessarily by having sexual relations with a married woman, but simply by not being a good virgin. Take the priest. He is a dedicated virgin, a celibate committed to the service of the community. If he spends too much time self-pleasure seeking, if he won't acknowledge his community flock or even come down to make out a mass card for his parishioner, he is guilty of spiritual adultery. Dedicated to the community, he sins when he fails to serve (and so to love) the community.

So, too, with the single man or woman. Their freedom *from* marriage should lead them to a freedom *to* service. If they just loll around all day and live for themselves they are committing spiritual adultery also. Christianity is, above all, a religion of service to one's fellow man. Virginity gives a wider outlet for this fulfillment. Not to pursue such fulfillment is to deny the christian reason for virginity at all.

What about the teenage boy? Being a virgin should be the most natural state for him. He need offer no apologies for it. In his growing up years he is learning to serve the community. Mixing and relating to others, learning to give of himself freely since he is still without marriage obligations, developing a well-rounded personality which will make his final choice of life more meaningful—this is his virginity. He is not using the symbol of total givingness when he really can't give total givingness; he's not making the commitment that goes with intercourse when he's not ready for commitment. His virginity is part of his freely chosen efforts at his "disciplined and devoted delay." Being a virgin is not a sign that he's unmasculine or that he doesn't have what it takes. He *does* have what it takes, but he's saving it. He figures that the girl he marries deserves all of him and the complete gift of himself. He figures that the girl he marries deserves a boy whose early virginity developed his talents of loving, his capacity for self-control and his service to the community. Teenage virginity is growing up and learning to get along with the many before settling down with the one; it's a kind of practicing his givingness-ability on the community before he trusts his love to another in the permanent state of marriage.

Marriage. That's the other choice in life. Let's say a word about that. Ordinarily marriage is the logical vocation for those people who have proven their capacity for friendship, companionship and communication as we saw in the last chapter. Marriage is a creative life-long friendship in the sense that it helps each partner to grow as a good human being. It is creative, literally, in that their free and open sexual love will produce children.

I don't know if the average boy is aware of this, but the burden of a successful marriage weighs much more heavily on a couple today than ever before. In past ages, society itself compelled the couples to make a go of marriage. A man and woman and their children all worked together on the farm. Each member, from grandpop to junior, was necessary to make the family a financial success. This joint effort kept them together. A man and woman seldom if ever divorced one another in those days for the simple reason they could not afford to. He could not afford to lose all that free labor and she could not afford to lose her means of support. The parents themselves taught their kids what little book learning they needed to know. Religion was a strong factor that bound all the members together. Even their recreation down on the farm was taken together. In short, the way people lived seventy-five years ago helped bind them together in a very close, emotional and spiritual union.

Today things have changed. The family does not work together. Rather, only the father usually works and in a place far from home. Education is in the hands of the State or private institutions. Recreation is geared to separate the family, not unite it. There are very few recreations that an entire family can take together these days. Every one goes his own way. Religion too is personal and individualized and not a uniting factor in the family.

The upshot of all this is that society no longer conspires to keep the family together. On the contrary. With all the outside agencies invading the family it is easier for the members not to communicate too much with one another and far easier for divorce to occur. A woman who is divorced feels no shame today. She is accepted in society. She receives a good alimony and often works and makes as much or more than her husband. If the family of today is to stay together they can no longer lean on the external pressure of society, but must rest their marriage squarely on their inner convictions. As a Catholic boy the reader must be building up the following five convictions about marriage.

1. *Marriage is from the hand of God.* The Catholic boy must agree with the long line of tradition which has always held marriage sacred. Every civilization, both an-

cient and modern, has always connected the gods with marriage, has always felt that the marriage relationship was unique and of a concern to the Divinity. Only our own age wants to make marriage so natural and even obsolete. No, God is connected with marriage. It's from His hand and reflects His own inner life of self-donation, His Tri-une active loving-giving. When the Catholic marries he must know that he's fulfilling God's plan.

2. *Marriage is the place for sex.* We've spoken many times of sex as the great symbol of surrender and of mutual responsibility. Marriage is the place where surrender and mutual responsibility takes place and can flourish. Marriage is where the human relationship is sealed with sex and pledged with sex and supported with sex.

3. *Marriage is a sacrament.* The state of being married conveys grace. Marriage as a sacrament gives a mutual holiness as the two fulfill their vocation. Marriage is a sign of the union of Jesus and His Church as St. Paul tells us. Holiness as given directly by Christ in this sacrament flows from husband to wife, from wife to husband and from both to their children.

4. *Marriage is a vocation.* Marriage is a way of life, a real contribution to society and civilization. Marriages not only share in the very creative power of God Himself, but they have the high duty of creating and daily re-creating children: their bodies and minds, emotions and consciences. This is a large job. It is a vocation.

5. *Marriage is forever.* We won't go into all of the problems of difficult marriages. We just wish to say that, ideally, marriage is for keeps: for better, for worse, until death. This foreverness is not something the Catholic Church has imposed from without; it's something that the

lovers themselves have imposed from within. You can't imagine a boy telling a girl, "Marry me and I will love you for three years, nineteen hours, eight minutes and twelve seconds!" No, every boy and girl speak of foreverness and pledge their love "from here to eternity." They would, in fact, be gravely insulted if anyone suggested that their love was good for just so many miles and then it would give out. They would be insulted if you asked them, "And how long do you intend to stay married?" Again, marriage as forever is *their* wish, *their* desire and *their* promise.

This book is not intended to be a treatise on marriage. I can only refer you to some excellent books and make one recommendation. Good books on marriage for the Catholic boy are: *Understanding Marriage,* by Charles and Audrey Riker (Deus Books). *Two to Get Ready,* by Rev. Henry Sattler and the books by Pierre Dufoyer, *Marriage, A Word to Young Men* and *Marriage, A Word to Young Women.* The one recommendation I would make is, when you are ready to get married, be sure to make the Pre-Cana conferences. These are usually five sessions given by a priest, doctor and married couples. They are very helpful in getting ready for marriage. Some parishes have made them mandatory.

The closing comment we would make about marriage is that it is intended to be and often is a beautiful fusion of two lives into one. It's the state where so many, going into it with all of their little self-cares and self-loves, emerge concerned only about the other. It's a state of constant interaction which hurts because the sharp corners of selfishness are being rubbed off, because the easily bruised pride is being subdued, because the self-centered heart is being broken. But in the process one becomes *real*. We've all witnessed golden jubileeans who had eyes only for one another. They have traveled the road from arrogant, selfish persons to humble selfless and real human beings. Life-long love and that alone has achieved this miracle. Perhaps it might be fitting to close with the conversation of two fairy tale figures. In her timeless and delightful children's book, *The Velveteen Rabbit,* Margery Williams has the Velveteen Rabbit asking what is REAL? The first one to give an answer is another toy, the old Skin Horse. He says:

> "Real isn't how you are made," said the Skin Horse. "It's a thing that happens to you. When a child loves you for a long, long time, not just to play with, but REALLY loves you, then you become Real."
> "Does it hurt?" asked the Rabbit.
> "Sometimes," said the Skin Horse, for he was always truthful. "When you are Real you don't mind being hurt."
> "Does it happen all at once, like being wound up," he asked, "or bit by bit?"
> "It doesn't happen all at once," said the Skin Horse. "You become. It takes a long time. That's why it doesn't often happen to people who break easily, or have sharp edges, or who have to be carefully kept. Generally, by the time you are Real, most of your hair has been loved off, and your eyes drop out and you get loose in the joints and very shabby. But these things don't matter at all, because once you are Real you can't be ugly, except to people who don't understand."[19]

Marriage makes people Real.

CHAPTER X

Homosexuality

"Harry" said the man coming home from work to his house. "Harry, all the guys at the office are calling me queer and odd. They keep saying that I'm a homosexual. They make me so mad! In fact, one guy made me so mad that I threw my lipstick at him!" This old joke pretty much sums up a lot of old and unreasonable attitudes about homosexuality. But homosexuality is like that: it carries a great deal of interest for the average person and at the same time it provokes a great deal of hostility and the spread of misinformation. Without trying to prejudice this chapter I was going to entitle it "Fairy Tales" with some pun intended since "fairy" is a nickname like "fag" and "queer" and "gay" for the homosexual. But I would have meant the title "Fairy Tales" in a wider sense because there is much fiction believed as fact about homosexuality; there's a lot of make-believe about it. Fairy tales exist on both sides: those who are "normal" tell them and those who are homosexual tell them. Let's try to see what we really know about homosexuality and what should be the Catholic boy's attitude about it.

Homosexuality is a sexual attraction to members of one's own sex. A person is physically stimulated and drawn to members of his own sex much the same way that the opposite sexes stimulate and draw each other. Homosexuality may include, therefore, a lack of sexual

138

attraction and desire for the opposite sex, even a certain basic fear of the opposite sex. Homosexuality, in its widest application, means any physical, sexual activity with members of the same sex. Statistics on how many people are homosexual are not accurate and guesses vary. Some say 3% of all human beings are homosexual; some say 5%. The famous Kinsey report in 1948 speculated that there are anywhere from two to three million homosexuals in the United States.

In this country homosexual acts are considered legally wrong and all states except Illinois provide jail sentences for offenders. Illinois, like Great Britain, allows homosexual activities between two consenting adults—although never between an adult and a minor. Much of our laws about punishing homosexual activity stems from our Jewish-Christian heritage. The ancient Jews from the sixth century B.C. had strict ideas about sex and forbade homosexual activity. The story of Sodom and Gomorrah in Genesis, Chapter 19, is often interpreted as a condemnation against homosexuality. St. Paul uses strong language in Romans 1:24-27 when he says there:

> That is why God left them to their filthy enjoyments and the practices with which they dishonor their own bodies, since they have given up divine truth for a lie and have worshipped and served creatures instead of the creator who is blessed forever. Amen! That is why God has abandoned them to degrading passions: why their women have turned from natural intercourse to unnatural practices and why their menfolk have given up natural intercourse to be consumed with passion for each other, men doing shameless things with men and getting an appropriate reward for their perversion.

From such a background come our present day restrictions and punishments about homosexuality. Let us see whether homosexuality deserves such a bad name and what are its causes.

First of all, there is considerable evidence that many boys just before adolescence and into its early years engage in some occasional sex play with other boys. While this sort of thing is not morally good, this does not mean that such boys are homosexual or will become so. Usually it means that boys at this age are often curious about the size and shape of their own sexual organs and those of other boys. They may solve this curiosity by "goosing" one another or grabbing at one another's sexual organs in horse play or even on occasion masturbating one another. Such occasional actions, while undesirable, do not necessarily fix a boy as a homosexual. Another thing we should know is that there is a little of homosexuality in all human beings. It is a common experience for many boys to be aroused by or feel affection for another boy one time or another. If a boy has some curiosity about another boy or some sexual fantasies or daydreams that include other boys, this is not something to be alarmed at if it is not a constant and long standing condition.

What causes homosexuality? Curiously (and we'll continue to speak only of male homosexuals for the moment) no one knows for sure. No one has the complete answer. There are a lot of guesses, but no definite conclusions. Here are some theories:

1. Some people would say that "homosexuals are born that way." They have different glands or chemicals or what have you. As far as I know, this is not true although some experiments give some evidence of some possible

chemical or biological predisposition. No, the common opinion is that homosexuals are made, not born.

2. Some would say that sometimes a boy's sexual yearning for another boy develops because he is afraid of girls. Maybe he's had some bad encounters with girls early in life. Whatever the reason, he has a fear of girls and an anxiety about them. Thus he may turn to boys as the object of his affection—and stay that way.

3. Sometimes boys get involved in sex with other boys and get stuck that way simply because boys are more available than girls! He can be with other boys all the time, go "skinney-dipping" with them, shower with them and sleep with them. He gets undressed with other boys before and after the game and has gym with them. In other words, sometimes the overwhelming opportunity gets a boy involved in sex with other boys.

4. Some boys get introduced to homosexual acts by men or older boys. Some doctors say that such boys may get to like this and enjoy it so much that they never graduate to an interest in girls and a desire for sex with them. This getting fixed at a certain stage can happen especially when a boy is very young and just starting to sexually develop.

5. The most commonly held theory is that boys are made homosexual by their family background, by the influence of their parents. The parents don't bring this about on purpose, of course, but they cause it nevertheless. This theory says that a bad combination of parents is what the doctors call a "C-B-I" mother and a physically or emotionally absent father or a hostile father. That "C-B-I" mother refers to "Close-Binding-Intimate" mother, that is, one who is very close to her son and binds him to

her by over-protecting and over smothering him. She "moms" him to death as it were, babies him all the time, won't let him grow up. This wouldn't be so bad if there was the strong, masculine figure of a father to offset this seduction. But if the father is absent or hostile to his son, then the mother's influence wins out and the boy, while all genuine boy on the outside, becomes a "girl" on the inside—in his mind and heart. As an "inside" girl he will naturally have an attraction to the "opposite sex," a boy. A Dr. Bieber and his associates who have studied the subject of homosexuality for many years go so far as to say this:

> The father played an essential and determining role in the homosexual outcome of his son. In the majority of instances the father was extremely hostile . . . we have come to the conclusion [that] a constructive, supportative, warmly related father precluded the possibility of a homosexual son; he acts as a neutralizing protective agent should the mother make seductive or close-binding attempts.[20]

The father, in this theory, seems to be the key figure. When you think of it, with the fathers these days being absent either by divorce or simply by working far from home or commuting or traveling all over the world, it *is* harder for boys to imitate a masculine figure, harder to know what "masculine" is. And mother? Well, understandably, she has to take over so many chores and oversee her sons much more today. She is likely to be the disciplinarian, drive the kids to the ball game, cub scouts, boy scouts, run the PTA and fight with the little league umpire. Going to school doesn't help either since a boy is likely to have female teachers for eight or more years of his life. With father being so absent and females being so dominant, it's no surprise that boys could pick up the feminine mentality.

That the family really influences a boy and the father's role is rather important for him is further brought out in a recent study by Dr. Urie Bronfenbrenner in the *Saturday Review of Literature,* called "The Split Level Family." Although not especially treating of homosexuality, the general influence of the absentee father is brought out quite well:

> Some relevant studies have been carried out in our own society. For example, I, with others, have done research on a sample of American adolescents from middle-class families. We have found that children who reported their parents away from home for long periods of time rated significantly lower on such characteristics as responsibility and leadership. Perhaps because it was more pronounced, absence of the father was more critical than that of the mother, particularly in its effects on boys. Similar results have been reported in studies of the effects of father absence among soldiers' families during World War II, in homes of Norwegian sailors and whalers, and in Negro households with missing fathers, both in the West Indies and the United States. In general, father absence contributes to low motivation for achievement, inability to defer immediate for later gratification, low self-esteem, susceptibility to group influence and juvenile delinquency. All of these effects are much more marked for boys than for girls.[21]

I make a point of this because the theory that a father-mother role is responsible for causing homosexuality is the most common one. Also I want to emphasize this theory to any fathers who may be reading this book.

6. A variation of the theory just described says that
it's not so much the overprotective mother or the cold
hostile father which produce a homosexual son, but
rather the violent interaction between them that does this.
The mother, for example, if she does not get affection
from her husband, will seek it overmuch from her son.
Or, if the father or mother can't communicate with each
other, they tend to use the child as an outlet for their
frustrations and so harm his emotional development. If
they both seek to "win" their son and try to get adult affection from him, they are seeking from him what he cannot give; he becomes an "emotional football" between
them. Instead of being really wanted by his parents for
himself, he is being used and that throws his inner approach to life out of whack.

Anyway, whatever makes him that way, whatever the
theory, the homosexual exists. He's a loner. He finds himself unable to communicate with others. He soon learns
to think of himself as "different" or "queer" and can't
seem to find acceptance or love. He becomes a disturbed
person. He is the fearful or lonesome boy who cannot re-
late to other boys well, who feels himself to be an outcast,
an outsider. If his homosexuality is apparent or obvious
or in some way becomes known, he meets with prejudice
and scorn. At times he meets with positive hostility from
the rest of us who are unwilling to admit that we have
some feminine ways in our hearts and minds, that we har-
bor homosexual feelings to a degree, and his open homosexuality threatens our secret. He begins to feel doomed
and he often cries out in anger at Fate or God or whatever or whoever played this trick on him. Is he condemned to live as a homosexual forever? The fear of

being told so prevents him from seeking help. His sense of isolation and queerness becomes a permanent factor. The homosexual may react to these pressures in various ways. He may turn to boasting of his condition and flaunting it; he may rationalize it and try to justify it; or he may simply despair and groan in frustration. In his book of a few years ago, *The Devil's Advocate* the author Morris West has the homosexual Nicholas Black say these words to Monsignor Meredith:

> I know your whole argument on the question of the use and misuse of the body. God made it first for the procreation of children and then for the commerce of love between man and woman. That's the end. All its acts must conform to the end and all else is sin. The sin according to nature is an act in excess of the natural instinct . . . like sleeping with a girl before you marry her, or lusting after another man's wife. To want a boy in the same fashion, is a sin against nature. . . . But there's the catch and here's what I want you to tell me. What about my nature? I was born the way I am. I was a twin. See my brother before he died and you'd have seen the perfect male—the excessive male, if you want. Me? . . . It wasn't clear what I was to be. But I knew soon enough. It was my nature to be drawn more to men than to women. I wasn't seduced in the shower room or blackmailed in the bar. This is what I am. I can't change it. I didn't ask to be born. I didn't ask to be born like this—God knows I've suffered enough because of it. . . .
>
> . . . But do I need love less? Have I less right to live in contentment because somewhere along the line the Almighty slipped a cog in creation? . . . What's your answer to that, Meredith? What's your answer for *me?* Tie a knot in myself and take up badminton and wait till

they make me an angel in Heaven, where they don't need this sort of thing any more? . . . I'm lonely! I need love like the next man! My sort of love! Do I live in a padded cell till I die? . . .[22]

This is the voice of homosexual anguish and frustration.

I said above that I was toying with the idea of calling this chapter, "Fairy Tales" because there is a lot of fiction given out about homosexuality on both sides: from the "straight" world and from the homosexual world. Let's start with the untruths such as the average citizen holds them.

1. *Homosexuality is confined to men.* This is not true since there is evidence that homosexuality among women is considerably higher. Homosexuality among women is called *lesbianism.* We are not as apt to be aware of this phase of homosexuality, however, since kissing and hugging and the like is commonplace among women; we think nothing of this. The same thing among men would arouse our suspicions. Like so much else in sex lesbianism is being talked about very much these days and portrayed in our novels and shown on our movie screens. Unfortunately these sources seldom handle the subject well and sensationalism rather than truth is presented.

2. *Homosexuals are the sissified, "fruity," feminine type of boy.* The stereotype of the young homosexual is the gay boy swishing down the school corridor with the walk and the airs of a girl. He may be a homosexual. He may not be. Or he is pictured as the boy who dresses up in girl's clothes (called "transvestism"). He may be a homosexual. He may not be. But certainly homosexuality is not confined to these types. Homosexuals can be found among football players and top sergeants. The body build

and facial image give no clue to the contrary. You *can't* tell a homosexual by looking at him.

3. *Homosexuals are met with in only certain callings.* This usually means that homosexuals are found only in the creative arts and in the theatre. This is not true. They are in other areas of life also—any area of life. It is true, I think, that they are found in the arts because the arts afford the solitude and the introversion that homosexuals need—something which may not be had in the busy, active, competitive, brusque masculine world. I have read somewhere that you can't get a dancing job on Broadway or on TV unless you're a homosexual. Although obviously exaggerated, there is probably some truth to this. But homosexuals are to be found in all walks of life.

These, then, are some of the "fairy tales," some of the lies or half truths about homosexuals. There are others, like every homosexual is out for sexual activity or homosexuals are fickle and unreliable or the rate of crime is higher among them than among others, etc. These statements need a great deal of qualification and correction and one ought not to believe them. On the other hand, as we said before, there are the "fairy tales" on the other side; that is, lies or half truths on the part of the homosexuals themselves. Here are some of them:

1. *Homosexuality is normal.* There are societies of homosexuals which try to get equal rights and equal privileges and equal considerations for homosexuals. These goals are good and praiseworthy. Some of these societies go too far, however. They wish to declare that homosexuality ought to be considered a normal way of life. They receive support from the general atmosphere today which says there are no fixed standards or absolutes. Yet, the

only way you can know what a crooked line is is to know what a straight line is. Sickness can only be known if you know what health is. So, too, with homosexuality. It is not normal in the sense of being common or in the majority or fulfilling the norm that opposite sexes attract and that the fusion of seed and egg produce human life. Homosexuality is not a disgrace—we'll speak more of this later—but neither is it "normal." I don't think it's a kindness to say that. I may feel sorry for the kid who's got one leg shorter than the other and I'll be a poor christian if I make fun of him and refuse my hand in friendship to him. But I'd be a poorer christian to say that his leg disproportion was normal or pretend that he was the same as the rest of the kids. Homosexuality is normal in the sense that it exists; it is not normal in the sense that it's the standard way of life for all. In his book, *The Sixth Man,* Jess Stern reports that, in the show-down, homosexual men admit that if they had sons, they would want their sons to be "straight" or non-homosexual.

2. *Because of their "condition" and their temptations, homosexuals should have unrestrained sex activity.* This bit of philosophy finds support from certain psychiatrists who preach that there should be no control for sex for anybody anyway. Sex is a basic animal instinct, they say, and you can't deny it. Even the married man is entitled to his affairs. This is not only nonsense, it is inconsistent. People who say this about sex do not say this about anything else whatever. Man has evolved not only from lower forms of life (this is what these people unhesitatingly believe) but his conduct and insights have evolved also. They all admit this. When people go to dinner they do not grab the food with their bare hands, crawl on the

table or slurp up the mashed potatoes. Although eating is
a real animal need, man has in the course of evolved time
attached much more to eating. He has, in fact, attached
great emotional feeling and intimacy with eating—and
this is progress. Eating has become social, ritualistic and
symbolic as well as biological. The tens of thousands of
restaurants and intimate eating places testify to this. Eating is filled with meaning and message and symbol.
Thanksgiving dinner at Grandma's, the little intimate
dinner for lovers, the wedding celebration, the birthday
party—all have come a long way from two animals fighting over a bone.

My point is this: everybody admits this is progress,
what we've described about eating. So, too, with every
other "animal" drive and instinct. We've become civi-
lized. Why, when it comes to sex, everyone wants to deny
that *it* has become meaningful too? No, they want us to
follow our instincts as we did ninety million years ago
and have sex when and where and with whom we can.
All of a sudden we're "back to nature" and the sex drive
has to have its discharge. Meaning, interpretation, symbolism, rules of etiquette and the rules of moral guidance
surround and invest all of our other "animal needs and
urges." Why do people except sex? Our old friend C. S.
Lewis had a point when he wrote slyly:

> When I was a youngster, all the progressive people were
> saying, "Why all this prudery? Let us treat sex just as
> we treat all our other impulses." I was simple-minded
> enough to believe they meant what they said. I have
> since discovered that they meant exactly the opposite.
> They meant that sex was to be treated as no other im-
> pulse in our nature has ever been treated by civilized

people. All the others, we admit, have to be bridled. Absolute obedience to your instinct for self-preservation is what we call cowardice; to your acquisitive impulse, avarice. Even sleep must be resisted if you're a sentry. But every unkindness and breach of faith seems to be condoned provided that the object aimed at is "four bare legs in a bed."

It is like having a morality in which stealing fruit is considered wrong—unless you steal nectarines. . . .

Our sexual impulses are thus being put in a position of preposterous privilege. The sexual motive is taken to condone all sorts of behavior which, if it had any other end in view, would be condemned as merciless, treacherous and unjust.[23]

No, the development or evolution from mere mating to a deep symbolism of sexual love between two human beings is a genuine advance. As a meaningful symbol the sex drive must be controlled and surrounded with guides and etiquette and rules—and this applies to the homosexual as well. Those who argue for the privilege of sexual sin for the homosexual would argue unchastity for the married man. True, homosexuals have more temptations. His taking a shower with the guys is like your taking a shower with girls. Imagine what a sweat you'd be in! But the homosexual must struggle for control like the rest of men; he may fall like the rest of men, but he must rise like the rest also. His "condition" gives him no exception from sincere efforts at chastity and sanctity. In the book, *The Invert,* the annoymous homosexual author says this:

Among the normal are saints and profligates. Between

those who have achieved sanctity and those who have chosen vice will be found the larger number, struggling sinners whose faltering progress is marked by many a pitiful tumble. Among inverts (homosexuals) there are saints and profligates, and between the extremes many who are struggling in a more or less successful attempt to follow the dictates of conscience and direction of authority.[24]

The author is saying that homosexuality deserves no special moral category. Like everyone else they must practice self control and chastity and make use of the same advice and spiritual aids.

What should be the Catholic boy's attitude towards homosexuality? First and foremost he must have Christ's attitude of love and kindness. "Love one another as I have loved you," Jesus said and this includes people who are "different." The life of the homosexual is basically a great and tremendous cry for love and understanding. If there's a kid in school the others dub as "queer" or a "homo," for the christian boy to join in this name-calling would be a grave fault against charity. If the kid really is a homosexual he'll need all the friends he can get. Don't be hostile towards him; don't be suspicious. If he's generally a decent guy he's not going to be impure with you. You can be a friend to him without guilt or fear. As I said, every homosexual cries for acceptance and love. Could you be a follower of Christ and refuse either?

Secondly, remember Jesus' other words, "Do not judge and you will not be judged because the judgments you give are the judgments you will get." How often the homosexual suffers from the prejudices and misunderstandings of others. If the Catholic boy really takes time out to understand him he can bring him closer to Christ who is his hope. Since, too, the homosexual is usually a loner, the hand of friendship will be of great benefit to him. You will be the "other" part of society making him feel welcome. More, you will be the Church giving him refuge.

With all of this being said, the rules of common sense for general well being must continue to be observed. As you ought not to flirt with strange women, so keep away from strange men and older boys. Homosexuality, like all things in life, has degrees. Some men will wink at a girl; those who are sick will attack, rape and kill her. There are all degrees to sicknesses, both physical and mental. So, too, with homosexuality. Many homosexuals are wonderful people with full control and stability; some are so disturbed that they will attack boys and even kill them. Some very disturbed homosexuals may hang around men's toilets looking for someone; others approach boys right on the streets or in dark alleys. The late Flannery O'Connor in her haunting book, *The Violent Bear It Away* describes how some man riding in his car picked up the book's hero, a young adolescent, gave him a drink with knock-out drops in it and the next thing the boy remembered was waking up in the woods with nothing on except his shoes. The man in the car had apparently misused his young body and handled his sexual organs. So, don't hitch-hike, especially alone. Don't go with strange men or boys particularly to their apartments or houses where no one is home.

A final personal note to you, the reader. Remember two things. First, involvement in any homosexual activities on your part in the past is not fatal in that they have made you a homosexual or prove that you are one. You're not doomed to this way of life for that reason alone. Secondly, homosexual feelings and attractions at certain periods of your life are often normal enough and are no cause for alarm. If, on the other hand, attraction to other boys persists, day dreams and sexual feelings about other boys persist and so make you worried and concerned, please discuss this with someone older like your parish priest. Often a couple of conversations can relieve your fears and apprehensions. Finally, if by any chance a boy has really and persistently engaged in homosexual activities, really is a homosexual but truly wants to change and is willing to do whatever he can to change his way of life, then there is very good hope for him. He can be helped. Perhaps he can even be cured; perhaps not. But in any case, there is hope of his living a good and adjusted life, of rendering a genuine contribution to society. To lock the door on one's "secret" is the worst thing a boy can do; to unlock it for at least one understanding and counseling adult is the first step to freedom.

CHAPTER XI

Contraception and Venereal Disease

1. CONTRACEPTION

Contraception or birth control is so much in the news that even a book on sex for Catholic boys justifies some comment and some information about it. The word contraception is its own explanation. It literally means "against conception" and so refers to the preventing of children being born from sexual intercourse through the use of any means from physical devices to internal medicines or drugs.

With what you know from the first two chapters about male and female anatomy you can almost figure out the kinds of contraceptives there might be. In general they would be designed to keep the man's seed from reaching the female egg or even keeping the woman's egg from appearing at all. Thus contraceptives fall into two main categories: those which interpose a mechanical or chemical barrier between the egg and the seed and those that prevent the egg from appearing or from developing (the pill or other drugs). Some of the common types of devices and pills are listed here:

1. *The Diaphragm.* This is an appliance which covers the entrance to the womb. It is made of soft rubber or similar material and has the shape of a shallow cup. This fits snugly into the woman's vagina and so blocks the en-

trance to the womb—the cervix; thus the male seed cannot enter. Another variation of this is the cervical cap which covers the cervix for the same purpose.

2. *Creams or jellies.* There are creams or jellies that contain powerful chemical agents (like an insecticide) which kill or immobilize the male seed. In addition, some of these creams or jellies form a foam over the entrance to the womb and so prevent the seed from getting in. This cream or jelly can come in a suppository form; that is, in the form of a small "popcycle" that melts with the body temperature in the vagina and so releases the chemicals.

3. *The Intrauterine Ring (IUD).* This is a kind of coil introduced within the cavity of the womb and prevents pregnancy. No one quite knows why but it has proven effective.

4. *The condom or "rubber."* This is a common device for the male to wear. It is a rubber sheath which is slid over the erect penis like a rubber balloon. When the seed fluid is released it is caught into this rubber sheath and thus cannot even touch or enter the woman's body.

5. *The Pill.* This is the famous pill swallowed internally like an aspirin. This pill acts like an artificial chemical. When a woman is pregnant she manufactures a hormone or chemical which acts to prevent the formation of other eggs in her body. This is why a pregnant woman can't get pregnant. Now scientists have developed this same hormone artificially. When a woman takes this artificial hormone (the pill) she fools her body into thinking that she is pregnant and eggs are prevented from forming. There is some controversy over the safety and the side-effects of the pill. Scientists are also at work on a pill for men that would render their seed sterile or weak.

These are some of the major ways of preventing having children while at the same time having sexual intercourse. Generally our comments about all this must fall into two main divisions: Contraception for the unmarried and contraception for the married. Let us take a look at each.

I. *Contraception for the unmarried.* There is only one reason that unmarried people would use contraceptives or birth control: they want the intercourse without the baby. They want to be impure but not "get caught." They want the pleasure but not the responsibility. But we've seen in a previous chapter that there is a larger question here than just making the female hygienically safe. The larger question is, "What does sex say? Is it to be a discharge or symbol?" We saw what Dr. Halleck and Dr. Calerdone had to say about sex before marriage. Making the female incapable of producing children is not the issue, but making her human and a person and not just an object of lust is. Saving the female and saving the act of intercourse as a great seal and symbol of dedication and loyalty and total donation is important. Choosing the "disciplined and devoted delay" of the sex drive honors any girl more than the mere discharge of a sexual urge without commitment. Contraception for the unmarried provides "safe" sexual intercourse but unsafe human relationships.

With the pill and other contraceptives girls especially are under heavy pressure to "go all the way." With pregnancy no longer a fear, why not have sexual intercourse before marriage. Dr. Halleck describes it this way:

> More girls may not be indulging in premarital intercourse, but more girls feel pressured to do so.
> The mass communication media in our country have a tendency to emphasize the most extreme forms of social

behavior and to present them as the norm. Our students receive a heavy bombardment of *Playboy* philosophies which argue for the enjoyment of sex for the sake of physical pleasure alone. Even our religious leaders are modifying their pleas for rigid adherence to premarital chastity. Our youths seem to have accepted a number of questionable beliefs which serve to perpetuate these pressures. For example, many of the girls I have spoken to believe that physical frustration per se is psychologically unhealthy. . .

Many girls also fear that denying their sexual charms to boys is a sign of selfishness . . . Not infrequently the girl who retains chastity is accused of emotional coldness, of not trying to be an open person. Finally, most girls believe that there is more sexual activity taking place than is actually the case. If they do not participate, they see themselves as atypical and strange.[25]

There are, then, heavy pressures put on the young to have pre-marriage intercourse, especially since contraceptives have made it "safe" to do so. Some modern parents practically push their children into sexual activity by giving them contraceptives before they go out on a date. In her daily column, "Dear Abby" published a letter from a modern mother who gave her 16 year old daughter the pill for her own (the mother's) peace of mind. Some of the letters responding to this were interesting. One said: ". . . if a mother raises her daughter right, she won't need the pill. This may come as a shock to you, but I am a 19 year old virgin. I'm no creep either." This modern mother's excuse for giving her daughter the pill was that if the "right" man came along and the time is right and the place is right, Lord knows what would happen. One writer replied to this by saying, "I would like to say that if a mother raises her daughter with high moral standards, when the right boy comes along, the right place will be the bridal chamber and the right time will be the wedding night. Don't faint, this is from a 21-year old college man."

Contraception for the unmarried is total safety all right. It's not only safety from getting pregnant, but safety from being committed; the girl is made "safe" from genuine human relationship and human care. When she protects herself from the fruitful intercourse of her unmarried boy friend she is also "protecting" herself from his responsible love.

2. *Contraception for the married.* Here we have a different situation altogether. The married couple are committed; responsibility has been taken, the public declaration of love has been made. This is not intercourse outside of commitment; this is sexual love *within* the commitment. May they use contraceptives? The general answer, according to Pope Paul's encyclical, *Human Life* is no. To disturb such a loving act is wrong; to inhibit it, frustrate it, deliberately to make it empty is a moral wrong. However, the use of contraceptives for the married is not always a sin. This is so, at least for what reason I can explain here, because no other recourse is left and contraception is resorted to, though not as a way of life. For instance, as a Father Chirico points out, there are three basic values in married life. One is the personal relationship between this husband and wife which is often conveyed by sexual intercourse. Another is the begetting of children and the third is raising and educating the children. Frequently all three values can be met and maintained. Sometimes they cannot. For example, maybe hav-

ing another child would hurt the third value: parents couldn't support the rest of the children. Maybe having another baby would endanger the mother's health; then who would take care of the husband and the other children? If on the other hand a couple decides not to have any more children by not having sexual intercourse, then they may hurt their own love and its expression and grow cold to one another. What do they do? They must try their best. They refrain from sex when possible. They may use the "Rhythm" system; that is, confining their sexual relations to those times of the month when the woman is not likely to conceive a child since there is no egg presently in her womb. They must sincerely try all these things and sincerely try to keep the balance of the three values of married life. There are cases however, when nothing works to keep the balance but using contraceptives. The couple who do resort to their use, as long as they realize that this is not the best and the most moral way to prevent children, as long as they realize that a genuine value is being hurt (much against their will) then although they are doing wrong, they do not sin. Contraception for them is building their love (even though in a defective manner) to strengthen their initial commitment. This is a far cry from the boy and girl who are uncommitted and are using contraceptives, not to strengthen and preserve other values, but solely for pleasure and completely outside of the context of married life.

2. VENEREAL DISEASE (VD)

Venereal disease is a highly contagious disease; it is transmitted only by some kind of sexual contact, mostly by sexual intercourse. But other sexual contacts can spread it such as any application of the sexual organs to any opening in the body, for example, the mouth or the rectum. There are several kinds of venereal diseases but the most common are gonorrhea and syphilis. As we said, veneral diseases are highly contagious and have increased among young people between 15 and 19 years of age. The alarming increase of this disease among the young is of great concern to the professional health officers. It is interesting to note that the United Nations World Health Organization (WHO) in a report of the Health Problems of the Adolescent held in Geneva in 1964 presented a statement of the problem of venereal diseases among the young and listed the following as the causes of the spread and increase of this disease:

1. Ignorance of the nature and meaning of sex and of the dangers and abuse of the sexual function.
2. The decline in religious faith.
3. The emancipation of women.
4. The lack of discipline in home life and of parental supervision.
5. The failure of fear as a deterrent.
6. The emphasis on sexuality in books, plays, and films, on television and in advertisements.
7. Misinterpretation of psychological teaching.
8. Earlier physical development.[26]

The effects of venereal diseases can be severe and even deadly. According to a pamphlet put out by the U. S. Department of Health, Education and Welfare syphilis can cause: insanity, paralysis, blindness, deafness, heart disease and death. Gonorrhea can cause: damage to the sexual organs, sterility, arthritis, blindness and death. This same pamphlet reminds us that venereal diseases can be transmitted only by sexual contact. It says:

> Syphilis and gonorrhea do not just "happen" to a person. They are not spread by water, food or air. They are NOT caught from toilet seats, door handles, drinking fountains, or eating utensils. They are NOT caught by lifting heavy things or straining. They ARE caught from persons who have them—through sex relations or close body contact.
>
> Just because a person has one of these diseases does not mean that he cannot have the other. He may have both at the same time. Or he may get cured and catch the same disease again if he is exposed to someone who has it.[27]

Venereal diseases are hard to detect because their symptoms vary and do disappear very quickly, but a person can have these diseases for years and years until they catch up with him and cause one or more of the illnesses described above. Let's take a look at gonorrhea and syphilis.

If a boy has sex relations with a girl who has gonorrhea, then in a few days or about a week he'll start to notice a kind of burning sensation when he urinates. Shortly after the boy may notice a small drop of pus discharging from his penis. These are the signs of this type of venereal disease. For the girl, on the other hand, she almost never notices any pain or other signs that she has this disease and, if she is impure, she can pass her disease on to as many boys as she has intercourse with. She does not even feel sick and there's no sign of the disease until it begins to spread through her womb and up the fallopian tubes. Then she does feel terrible pain; she may have to go to a hospital for treatment, perhaps even an operation —and then she may not be able to have children.

Gonorrhea is curable. Formerly it could be cured only by a long and sometimes quite uncomfortable treatment. Today a shot of penicillin or one of the sulfa drugs will cure gonorrhea. If the gonorrhea is not treated it will continue to spread and endanger the boy. However, gonorrhea, like syphilis, is sneaky. Its symptoms of burning and the drop of pus will disappear eventually and perhaps fool the boy into thinking that it has gone away. This is not true. It's there but it's hidden and will cause great harm later on.

Syphilis affects boys and girls the same way. The syphilis germ enters the body through the skin around the moist parts of the body: the penis, vagina or mouth. The first sign of syphilis may be a sore which may occur on the penis or vagina. This sore is known as a "chancre" (shan'-ker) and appears about sixty days after infection. This sore will disappear in time again fooling the boy or girl into a false security. Later, after the sore has disappeared, a rash will show up. It can be so light, like a heat rash, that it will not be noticed or paid attention to. This rash may cover the body or be just on the hands or feet. Sores may appear in the mouth. Sore throat, fever or headache may develop. Hair may even fall out in patches in this stage of the disease's development. But again, all of these signs will disappear in time and the person may feel relieved and once more deceive himself that he doesn't have this disease. Syphilis can harm the unborn baby. The father cannot pass on his disease directly to the baby, but he can give it to the mother who can. Such a baby may be born prematurely. It may be born dead or deformed or even born with hidden syphilis which will attack the child in some way later on.

Syphilis, like gonorrhea, can be cured by a series of penicillin shots. Still, with the cure at hand, veneral diseases continue to rise among the young and the young either do not recognize the symptoms or else are unwilling to go for treatment. This unwillingness to go for treatment is understandable (though foolish) for the only way a boy can get venereal diseases is by being impure with another person (boy or girl) and he will have to admit this to the doctor. Moreover, since these diseases are so highly contagious, the doctor will have to know the name of his partner or partners. This is most important because boys and girls who have sexual relations tend to have them with more than one partner and one boy or one girl can be the cause of spreading the infection to thousands of people. The doctors *must* track down the carrier of these diseases if they're ever going to conquer them.

It is interesting to realize that venereal diseases, like most human problems, are solved or at least prevented by good morality. The pure boy can never, never catch these diseases. Learning about sex is not learning "how-to-do-it" techniques or how to have sexual intercourse. Anybody can learn that in a half an hour. Learning about sex is learning about *people* and about loving them properly and how to have genuine human relationships with them. It is noteworthy that all of the secular and public sources on sex education come back again and again to *moral* training in the conquest of venereal diseases, illegitimacy and the like. The Government pamphlet we referred to above ends its paper with these words:

> Most important of all VD—and the promiscuity behind

its current upsurge—is a problem of morality, of a
breakdown in established values, that is of mounting
concern to clergymen, educators and sociologists. When
the public-at-large decides to treat VD as a moral issue,
the problem will largely be solved.

The World Health Organization report referred to
above also says this:

It is certainly desirable that children should know the
broad facts of sexual relationships considerably before
puberty. If the parents are unable to give the necessary
instruction they should authorize some suitable person
whom the child holds in high regard—such as a minister
of religion, a school teacher, or some near relative—to
deputize for them. The teaching of biological facts, however, is not a substitute for discussion of the moral and
emotional aspects of the problem. Training of will and
character is the proper function of education and up-
bringing and if this has been neglected practical information about the sex act and the problems arising from it
can add little or nothing.

CHAPTER XII

Questions, Answers and Glossary

In this chapter I want to answer some of the questions that were not raised in the course of the book. At the end of these questions and answers I will include a glossary of terms that will help in your general reading.

1. *Are some boys more "sexed" than others?*

Yes they are. Just like some boys are more nervous than others, more alert, more sensitive, more prone to sickness, more quick-tempered. So, too, a boy may have a more responsive "sexual" system. He may be an early or late developer as we saw in chapter one. His interest in and response to sex depends on many factors.

2. *Can a girl get pregnant without actually having intercourse?*

Yes she can, but this would be rare. Remember we said that the male seed has a tail that propells it throughout the female system in search of an egg? If a boy's seed fluid is discharged on the girl's thigh it is possible for some of the seed to move up and into her body through the vagina and so get her pregnant.

3. *How long does sperm or seed live?*

Seed can live in the vagina up to three days.

4. *What is an illegitimate child*

An illegitimate child is one who is born of people who are not married. Another term for illegitimate is "bastard." You think this is a "dirty" word, but it's quite ordinary and technical; you'll find it in the Bible (Goliath, for instance) and in Shakespeare. The thing to remember, however, is that the term "illegitimate" child is not quite proper as if the child were no good or evil or less than human. The illegitimacy really belongs to the parents. *They* made sexual love without taking the responsibilities of married life. *They* are guilty, not the child. The child can grow up to be a great saint.

5. *What is circumcision?*

Circumcision is cutting away the loose piece of skin that overlaps the end of the boy's penis. Often the doctor will cut it away shortly after the baby is born. This seems to be the common practice today for all baby boys. With this loose skin gone it's easier to keep the tip of the penis clean.

6. *What is an ejaculation?*

Ejaculation is a term to describe the spurting out of the male's seed fluid; to ejaculate is to discharge this seed fluid.

7. *What are adultery and fornication?*

Technically, adultery is having sexual intercourse and one or both of the partners are married—but not to each other. Fornication refers to having intercourse when neither is married.

8. *What is a prostitute or whore?*

A prostitute or whore (pronounced "Hoar") is a girl or woman who has sexual relations for money. She gets paid to be used.

9. *What is rape?*

Rape means "to snatch" or take by force. Rape, therefore, is forcible intercourse. A man or boy forces himself on a girl; he makes her have intercourse against her will. A genuine comment on this would be to observe that this is an ultimate or high point of selfishness. A boy thinks of sex totally as a discharge and when the urge is on him he must have it whether with an old grandmother or little girl. There is not even tenderness with the rapist. He wants what he wants and when he wants it. Outside of mental illness, a rapist is made not born. He feeds his life on sexual nonsense, practices no self-control and so attacks and even kills so enslaved is he to the sexual drive.

10. *What should the Catholic boy do who is scrupulous about sex?*

There are some boys who are extra sensitive about sex and feel they're committing sin whenever they have something to do with sex. They were probably influenced by a nervous parent or an extra-sensitive parent. Sometimes parents start early scrupulosity about sex if they convey disgust or shame with the sexual organs, like slapping the baby boy's hands if he's handling his penis and saying "dirty" or "shame" or the like. The best thing for the boy is to bring his questions to a priest and to go over ideas such as are contained in Chapter 3 on sexual joy.

11. *What should a Catholic boy do if he's in mortal sin but has to go to communion?*

A not uncommon case would be a boy who's masturbated on Saturday night and goes to Mass on Sunday with his parents who expect him to go to Holy Communion. Or he's going to Communion with a group or his graduation class, etc. What should he do? The best thing is to make a good act of contrition and go to Communion. Then, the next time he goes to confession, he should make mention of his procedure.

12. *What is impotence?*

This term refers to the inability to get an erection. At times it may also refer to being unable to discharge the seed fluid (ejaculate).

13. *What is sterility?*

Sterility is the condition where either the male or female is incapable of producing children. When this is accomplished deliberately, usually by an operation, it is called *sterilization.*

14. *What is abortion?*

Abortion is deliberately ending a pregnancy, causing the death of the unborn life.

15. *Are there foods or drugs that will either increase or decrease the sexual drive?*

In spite of much talk to the contrary there is no evidence that certain drugs or foods pep up or slow down the sex drive.

16. *What is incest?*

Incest is having sexual intercourse with one's relatives.
A boy having intercourse with his sister, mother, etc.
would be committing incest.

17. *Are girls tempted about sex too?*

Yes they are. But not in the same way boys are. They
have curiosity about sex but they are not drawn to it as
boys are. A girl would much prefer a little TLC (tender
love & care) than actual physical sex. She looks for security and love. Sometimes she "puts up" with sex or uses
sex to get this.

18. *Is it true that girls are slower to arouse than boys?*

Yes. Remember boys produce millions of seeds all the
time while girls have only one egg that ripens a month.
This contrast points out the excitability of boys and girls.
To exaggerate somewhat, if it takes a girl about a half
hour to get sexually aroused, it will take a boy about a
second! This is why we often—and perhaps unfairly—
place the burden on the girls to stop things before they go
too far. Since she takes longer to get "worked up" she has
more time and more opportunity to check the boy who
gets aroused so easily. Something which few girls ever appreciate, by the way, is this quick excitability of the boys.
She is apt to mistake the boy's passion for affection and
he's apt to take her affection for passion—and that's
when they get into trouble.

19. *Do girls need sex education too?*

They certainly do! And, as we said above, they need to
learn more about boys. When you see some girl pawing a

boy and rubbing his back or sitting on his lap or hugging him tightly—you know she's giving him trouble and you suspect that she really doesn't realize it. If you say something to her, she's often perplexed. *She's* not getting excited so she sees nothing wrong with what she's doing. Wearing a brief brief bikini, wearing a tight sweater, wearing a mini skirt, these things don't bother her so she fails to see the problems and the temptations she's giving boys. She needs education.

20. *How about "bad" girls who really try to get a boy?*

Usually a young sexy girl who practically throws herself on boys and dresses and acts to arouse them hurts a lot inside. If you'll notice she probably comes from a rather poor background; that is, her parents are divorced or separated or she has a stepfather she doesn't get along with or she's rejected at home or she's allowed to do whatever she wants—which is a form of rejection. With so much unconscious hurt *inside* her she tries to seek out some boy who will give her the affection and security she's missing. The only way she feels that she can attract boys is by being sexy. Unfortunately, she succeeds. She attracts the boys who are in the same boat and boys who exploit her sexually and then leave her. This type of girl is also a prime target for the going steady department. She would be highly insulted if you pointed out to her that unconsciously her steady date is her substitute father that she never had at home!

21. *If a boy gets a girl pregnant should he marry her?*

Most times, no. Especially if they are underage. Getting married fools nobody. Everybody can count up to nine and all the kids in school know that when a boy and girl who have been going steady drop out to get married that she's pregnant. If these kids were too immature to control themselves before marriage, marriage is not going to bestow maturity.

22. *What can a pregnant girl do if she doesn't marry?*

If she is a Catholic, she should see a priest or directly herself contact her local Catholic Welfare Bureau. Every diocese has one. It will be listed in the local phone book or the rectory will give you the number. The Welfare Bureau will see to it that the girl gets excellent mental and psychological attention and then have the baby put up for adoption. Putting the baby up for adoption sounds terribly cruel to most girls, but it really is the best thing. This way the baby will be raised in a normal, loving and mature household and have a chance in life. For the girl who is young to raise her child by herself or pass the child off as her brother or sister seldom works out well.

23. *Is the sexual act of intercourse always enjoyable and delightful?*

This is a good question, and the answer is "No." But we must distinguish between the *meaning* of the act and its actual *performance*. As we saw in the book, sexual intercourse is a great seal and symbol. It's a symbol of total donation and total surrender. It's a symbol of taking responsibility. As a symbol of such love sexual intercourse is always meaningful and always perfect. BUT—as a performance in reality, since it is a human act, it suffers from all the mistakes and all the imperfections that human beings are capable of. Perhaps a few examples may help. The kiss is a sign of respect, regard and affection. Ideally the kiss should convey all these meanings and does convey them. However, if in its meaning it is something good, in its performance it may be miserable. Suppose, for instance, the moment the boy is about to kiss his girl he suddenly sneezes right into her face! This is certainly a miserable and damp performance and should lead to instant disgust and later laughter. It just turned out that way and the boy and girl realize that something went wrong but at the same time realize that the kiss is still meaningful in spite of *their* experience with it. A wedding ring is a wonderful symbol of the endlessness of the husband's love (a round ring with no beginning and no end), a sign of his loyalty and fidelity and pledge. Still, the wife can catch her ring on a kitchen appliance and hurt herself; her hand can swell for some reason or another and the ring will give her pain. The ring perhaps can turn dull or dark. No matter. She knows that it has meaning regardless of what actually happens as she wears it. Take a valentine. Little Johnny says to Mommy, "Here, Mommy, I made you a valentine!" Indeed he did! It's uneven; in fact, it looks like he tore it into shape rather than used scissors. It has something scrawled on it which Mommy thinks says, "I love you." There's some mess on it and Mommy is almost sure Johnny's wiped his nose on it! But what does she do? She accepts it and is pleased sincerely. Why? Because Mommy knows that this messy, sloppy valentine has *meaning*. As a symbol it is perfect even though in actual reality it leaves much to be desired.

The same thing is true of the sexual act. As a symbol it

is perfect. It is one of the most complete ways to say "I love you." But it is human too. As such in reality, in actual performance, it can be most miserable. Little Susy may run into the bedroom crying for a drink of water just as Daddy and Mommy are to have intercourse. The husband may have to belch just as he's beginning the act. The wife may suddenly get a headache or one of the children may be sick and her mind's not on what she's doing. The husband might "come on" too soon; that is, he will ejaculate or discharge his seed fluid much too soon before he can insert his penis into his wife's vagina. There's a thousand things that could go wrong. If the couple realize that intercourse is a pledge, their "valentine" as it were, all of the wrong things won't matter and they won't really care. As long as intercourse is meant to say "I love you," so what?

Our problem is that the average boy and girl gets the impression from the movies and the novels that on each and every occasion each and every act of sexual intercourse is a profound, moving and hysterical experience lifting the couple into "seventh heaven." *No* human experience does that each time; why sex? If a couple is brought up on such lies and such trash they will be terribly disappointed with the reality and begin to accuse each other of all sorts of things. In his conversations the famous writer and publisher Frank Sheed refers to this nonsense as "holy copulation"; that is, everybody is supposed to discover human perfection here and that each act of sex is filled with ecstasy and grace. No, even Cape Kennedy has its duds. So does the act of sex. Keep the *meaning* pure and true; expect frequent disappointment in its *performance*.

24. *When a boy gets married does this mean he can have all the sexual relations he wants?*

No, not at all. Getting married doesn't give a boy a "green light" for uninhibited intercourse. As we indicated in the last question, intercourse is a human act and as such has limitations. The first steak is grand; the second helping is good, the third might leave you unimpressed and the fourth will make you throw up. Too much of anything, even a good thing, tends to repel after a while. So it is with sex. Too much and too often can rob it of its meaning.

Remember also that humans have Original Sin and can seek the sex pleasure for its own sake rather than sex as a symbol. If that happens a wife will begin to suspect that she's being "used" and not being loved for herself. Sex is a passion and can be demanding and gluttonous and overbearing. So in marriage sexual relationships must be "paced" in order to keep passion in check. It may interest you to know that some of the Orthodox Jews practice staying away from sex with their wives precisely to give themselves and their wives a time of rest and to revive the meaning and joys of sex when they resume sexual relations again.

Finally, there will be too many emotional and medical times which will require a husband's restraint from sex. A wife, for example, may not be feeling well. As we said above, she may be concerned about her sick child and can't give her attention to her husband at the moment. Near the end of pregnancy and just after childbirth husband and wife should not have intercourse. Separation, say, when the wife goes visiting or the husband is on a business trip will require restraint. So there's no such thing as free and uninhibited sex in marriage. Restraint and self-control have to be practiced for the married couple as for anyone else. It is important for boys and girls to set their mind to this beforehand. *And,* I might add, this is one of the very valuable side benefits from being pure before marriage; the ability at self-control gained before the wedding will be a tremendous help afterwards. By the same token, unrestrained sex before marriage argues for many a difficult time afterwards.

25. *Can you name me any good books on sex that will give me a good christian viewpoint?*

Yes, I can. There are several books that a Catholic boy could benefit from. I will list some of them here. I have marked an asterisk (*) before the ones I think that older boys could read with profit—say, from seniors in high school on up.

How You Were Born, by Robert P. Odenwald. P. J. Kenedy & Son, New York, 1962. An excellent text and good illustrations. If anyone is just beginning his sexual education, this is a good book and a simple one.

Two for the Road, by A. J. Bueltmann. This is part of the Sex education series put out by the Lutherans. All of the series is excellent. This would cover grades 7, 8 and 9. Published by the Concordia Publishing House, St. Louis, Missouri.

Life Can Be Sexual, by Elmer N. Witt. Same company and series as above. Great for high school kids.

Don't You Really Love Me?, by Joseph Champlin, Ave Maria Press. We referred to this in our book.

* *Sex, Love and the Person,* by Peter Bertocci, Sheed & Ward, New York, 1967. Very good for upper high school and college boys.

Why Wait Till Marriage?, by Dr. Evelyn Duvall. Referred to in our book. Put out by Association Press, New York, 1965.

A Christian Guide to Your Child's Sex Life, by Valerie Vance Dillon and Walter Imbriorski. Put out by the Cana Conference of Chicago, 1966. North Rush Avenue, Chicago, Illinois. Written for parents, but you can get a lot out of it too.

The Wonder of Sex, by Dr. and Mrs. Wilke, Hiltz Publishing Co., Cincinnati, Ohio, 1964. Like the book above, meant for parents but beneficial to you.

* *Shalom,* by Bernard Haring, Farrar, Strauss and Giroux, New York, 1967. Deals with moral questions and confession.

Dating for Young Catholics, by George A. Kelly, Doubleday & Co., Garden City, New York, 1963.

Glossary of Terms

Adolescence ....The period of time during which a boy and girl leave the neutral state of childhood and assume the physical, mental and spiritual tools of adult life.

Adultery ....Sexual relations between people who are married but not to each other.

Buttocks ....The part of the body you sit down on. The two large muscles below the back.

Cervix ....The neck or immediate entrance of the womb.

Chastity ....Accepting and controlling the sex drive in or out of marriage. The use of sex as God designed it.

Chromosome ....The thread-like material in the egg and sperm on which hang the genes or hereditary qualities.

Circumcision ....Cutting away the loose skin, called foreskin, around the tip of the male penis.

Clitoris ....A small penis-like organ of the female located within the vagina; the seat of sexual stimulation.

Conceive ....To begin a new life in the womb.

Contraception ......Preventing pregnancy while still having intercourse.

Contraceptives ......Any physical or chemical device, external or internal, which prevents having children.

Embryo ....The new life in the mother's womb up to eight weeks.

Excretion ....The solid waste matter passed off through the large intestine between the buttocks. Slang: "shit."

Fertilize ....The union of the male and the female reproductive cells to form a new life; to make pregnant.

Fetus ....The unborn baby after eight weeks in the mother's womb.

Fornication ....Sexual intercourse between two unmarried people.

Gene ....The unit of heredity.

Homosexuality ......The sexual desire, love for or activity with the same sex.

Illegitimate ....Refers to a child born of parents who are not married. Another term is Bastard.

Masturbation ....Handling of one's sexual organs; causing by oneself the erection of the penis and the discharge of the seed fluid. Also called "self-abuse."

Menstruation . . . . The monthly flow of blood from the womb.

Navel . . . . The place where the umbilical cord attached to the stomach. Slang: "belly-button."

Nocturnal emission . . The discharge of the extra stored up seed fluid at night, usually in connection with a "sexy" dream. Also called "wet dream."

Ovary . . . . The female sex gland.

Ovulation . . . . The process of an egg ripening in the ovary and dropping into the womb by way of the fallopian tube.

Ovum . . . . The female egg.

Penis . . . . The male finger-like sex organ. The organ through which the male urinates. His "contact" organ which joins him to the female in sexual intercourse.

Pituitary gland . . . . . . The "Master" control gland which regulates the action of the sex glands. Resides at the base of the brain.

Placenta . . . . A special network of blood vessels that develop on the lining of the mother's womb during pregnancy to which the umbilical cord runs exchanging waste matter from the baby and food and air from the mother.

Primary joy . . . . The free, spontaneous joys of the body which are normal and moral.

Procreation . . . . Literally, "to create-for" God; to beget children as a delegate for God.

Puberty . . . . The start of adolescence.

Pubic hair . . . . The coarse hair that grows around the sexual organs.

Rectum . . . . The opening between the buttocks; also called the anus.

Scrotum . . . . The external pouch or sac between a male's legs containing the two testicles.

Secondary joys . . . . . . Refers to all the deliberate joys of sex freely taken.

Sex . . . . The broad term referring either to the reproductive system of a person or his or her general "tooling."

Sexual intercourse . . . The penetration of the female vagina by the male penis with the release of the seed fluid. Also called coitus.

Sexuality . . . . The state of being a sexual person all over and all the time. One's personality given push and dimension by sex. A person's over-all "posture" in life as a male or female.

Sperm . . . . The male unit of procreation. Called the seed; the male contribution to the creation of the baby.

Testicles . . . . The male sex glands.

Umbilical cord . . . . . . The tube between the mother's placenta and the baby's stomach.

Urine . . . . The liquid waste matter.

Vagina . . . . The female opening between her legs which receives the male penis and also through which the baby passes at birth. Also called the birth canal.

Venereal disease . . . . A disease transmitted only by sexual contacts; a germ or virus which causes considerable damage to the one infected.

Virgin . . . . .One who has not had sexual intercourse.

Vulva . . . . .The external folds of flesh that surround the opening of the female vagina.

An Epilogue for Boys

Nobody likes comparisons, yet I can't help compare the time you're living in with the time that I grew up as a boy. My sympathy is with you. I think you have it so much tougher today than when I was your age. Oh, yes, we had our "sexy" jokes and our adolescent curiosity but beyond that, not much information otherwise. We just lived in a kind of happy ignorance but in a "protected" society free of wholesale sex and full of good and happy marriages (at least it seemed so to us at the time). Today —well, every place you go you're bombarded with all kinds of way out stuff about sex. Some of those TV shows can get to you, the movies ads are pretty exciting, the movies themselves are more explicit than ever, the sexy paperbacks are like a printed avalanche, the sexy magazines, both "girlie" and homosexual, are widespread— sometimes I think you'll drown in an ocean of sex. You've got a wealth of sex information but don't know what to do with it, how to interpret it, how to assess what it really means.

Besides leaving you somewhat confused, all of this sex business (publicized by the "advice" and carryings on of some pretty weird people) is going to make you think that purity is not only not the "in" thing any more, but an outright disadvantage. As we mentioned in the book, to be called a "virgin" or "wholesome" is like being called a dirty name. Anyone who really wants to observe chastity before marriage and faithfulness after marriage is made to feel odd, not quite masculine or feminine. In other words, to "go along with the crowd" is a stronger temptation than ever before.

And yet, if you're the average American boy, I have a
great deal of faith in you and in your common sense. I
have learned that you really want to be pure as do the
majority of kids. I have found the average boy decent
and honest. He may kid about sex and horse around
about it but in his heart he *knows* a lot of this sexy stuff is
nonsense and that it isn't really the way the movies or
Peyton Place tell it. Some, but not everybody is running
around with someone else's wife. Not every husband is
bedding down with his secretary. Not every boy is shack-
ing up with all the girls in his high school. People like
yourself and parents like yours make up the large majority of decent people who want to keep the laws of man
and God and want to observe the rules that can bring
them happiness.

A quick look at the lives of these kooky people should
make you pause anyway. They've got a long way to go to
prove that their free-swinging sexual affairs are really the
best and the happiest way to live. The Hollywood crowd
seem to change partners like their dirty socks in a constant merry-go-round of divorces. *Look* magazine once
quoted Nancy Sinatra as saying that even divorce can be
pleasant. It's hard to believe that. A divorce represents a
basic failure in human relationships A divorce may be
necessary, but *pleasant?* Can you pull back your body
and heart from another with no regrets, no sadness?
Look at the gorgeous sexpot Marilyn Monroe. She winds
up married several times and then killing herself. How
moving and how true were the words she spoke shortly
before she died. Something to the effect that she had become a symbol of sex, a thing, and she said "I just hate
being a thing!" How about the kids you know in high

school who "had" to get married and so shortened their own educational careers and cheated their own futures? What I'm trying to say is that the average boy like yourself feels that the loose and well publicized sex lives of the few still have a long, long way to go to convince you that their way of life is better than that "disciplined and devoted delay" which we mentioned in the book.

But even if the distorted and unhappy lives of such people didn't give us pause we still have several considerations to think about. First is the fact that as the average boy, you want to give the best of yourself to any girl and you want her to give her best to you. Well, after all, that's only natural and decent. If you love a girl you certainly feel that she's entitled to all of you, completely and totally. You want to share yourself with her and her alone. You want something unique between you. You want to build a life together without any past regrets. You desire to give her an unsoiled body and a clean heart. She deserves that much from you. You know that you want her to be a virgin when you marry her; that she has not shared her body intimately with another boy before you. You want the sex act to be yours and yours alone—your personal "I love you," your personal and private exchange of devotion and love. This in itself is an excellent reason for self-control and purity.

There's the second consideration. You are a *Catholic* boy. You know that as a follower of Christ you can't adopt everyone else's values. No, you must adopt the values of Christ Himself. You have to be different. So what? I would hate to think that all of your values whether about smoking, drinking, cheating, or sex were simply imposed on you by the others. I would hate to think that your character is being formed by the crowd and not by your own inner convictions. If the magazines tell you that being "manly" is to pet a girl, make out with her or have intercourse with her, you must not believe these things. At least not more than what Jesus tells you when He says to *love* your neighbor. If the movies get across to you that to be "manly" is to have muscles and a big body build, do not believe it. There are others, you know, (like Jesus) who feel that the real judge of manliness is not the strength of a boy's muscles but rather the strength of his character. There are those who feel that the real judge of manliness is not the amount of hair a boy has on his chest, but the amount of concern and compassion in his heart. The real boy, regardless of his body build and his sexual activity, is the local "Samaritan" who does for his neighbor ("Go and do likewise"), who gives food to the hungry and drink to the thirsty, who knows that it profits him nothing to go along with the crowd and gain the whole world but thereby suffer the loss of his own soul, his own integrity. As a Catholic boy the only pressure you should feel is the urgency of following Christ. "The love of Christ urges me on," cried St. Paul. So, too, the love of Christ must urge you to follow your own conscience even if the price is rejection; even, if it should ever be, death.

In his play of a few years ago, *A Man for All Seasons,* (later made into a movie) the author Robert Bolt shows us a man who would not give in to pressure even though it cost him his life, even though his "friend" coaxed him to go against his conscience. When all of his associates signed the Oath of Supremacy and upheld King Henry VIII's second marriage, Sir Thomas More would not. At his ap-

pearance before the Commission his friend Norfolk is
questioning him. The dialogue goes like this:

Norfolk: Oh, confound all this . . . I'm not a scholar, as
         Master Cromwell never tires of pointing out, and
         frankly I don't know whether the marriage was
         lawful or not. But, damn it, Thomas, look at those
         names. . . . You know these men! Can't you do
         what I did, and come with us, for fellowship?

More: And when we stand before God, and you are sent
         to Paradise for doing according to your conscience,
         and I am damned for not doing according to mine,
         will you come with me, for fellowship?[28]

There's a man for you, a man that history honors and admires. But you and I know that Thomas More, the man
of integrity, didn't become that way over night. Thomas
More started out as a boy of integrity. His strong manly
conscience was the result of a good adolescent conscience.

Finally, you are reminded by St. Paul that your body is
a Temple of the Holy Spirit and you ought not to dese-
crate that temple. Purity is self-respect, a kind of self-
honoring of the God Who is dwelling within you.

Remember, however, what else we told you in the
book. Christ does not expect you to hide in a closet all
your life and have *nothing* to do with sex. No, you live in
a real world and there are legitimate sexual pleasures and
encounters for the adolescent boy. We referred to these as
the "primary joys" of sex in the book. We encouraged
you to be proud you're a boy, to be pleased with your
body, to be happy with all of those free, spontaneous sexual joys that come your way. Like Jesus you live in a

world of people, of men and women, of boys and girls. It's your world and it's a sexual world and you must be a part of it. Not a part of sexual exploitation, but a part of sexual honor.

As I close this book, perhaps the best thing I can do is to leave you the example and the pattern of Jesus himself. St. Luke tells us in his Gospel that as an adolescent Jesus "grew in wisdom, age and grace before God and man." This should be your program too. *Wisdom.* This means that you give yourself to your present vocation which is that of a student. Regardless of your brain power, give yourself to study. Grow in as much knowledge and wisdom as possible. You're building for a future when you do so. I don't mean, either, a future job but I mean your future as a person, as a man. Being a student is a full time vocation. Try to be good at it.

But your wisdom must be exercised in other ways too. For example, being *able* to procreate a child doesn't mean that you are *ready* to do so. There's a great deal of preparation to get married. You must be financially ready, mentally ready, emotionally ready and finally, spiritually ready. As an average teenage boy you know you are not ready in all of these ways. You know it and your wisdom should lead you to take the steps that will both keep your sexual drives in check while you prepare yourself for adult living and marriage.

Age. This means that you are sexually developing. Having read this book you should be able to sit back and watch yourself grow and have a fine and open joy about your body and give thanks to Jesus after receiving Holy Communion for all the erections and all the sexy dreams you had that week. Age means that you recognize your sexual feelings, that they are indeed powerful as well as enjoyable. You know that you must be on your guard as a child of Original Sin. The temptation to self-abuse, the inclination to dishonor a girl will always be there. Learning control is a part of growing up.

Grace. Your spiritual life, your sacramental life must be a part of your adolescence. Go to Mass. So maybe you're bored and just stand in the back. But you're there. Just giving God your boredom, your tiredness, your doubts is a great act of worship. As you get older you will voice new criticisms of your religion, your faith, your church. Fine. This is a sign of stretching your mind. But in all of your mental growth and your physical growth try to keep close to God. Go to Communion and go to confession. We gave you some good advice about confession and warned you of the temptations of shame and hypocrisy you're liable to meet. No one ever won his battle without the grace of God. You'll be no different. Stay close to Jesus.

I indicated in the Introduction of this book to the adults that you would find some of the pages written above your level and so not easy to understand. Re-read the difficult passages. Better still, get some guidance and help in reading the book. Bring it to your priest or some adult whom you trust. Two heads are better than one and good adult guidance is a blessing to any boy.

May there be a blessing upon you who are reading this book, who are joyfully serious about things that matter. May you, like the teenage Christ, "grow in wisdom, age and grace before God and man."

NOTES

1. Luke 1:26 ff. Confraternity of Christian Doctrine translation. All other scripture quotations from the Jerusalem Bible.
2. Trimbos, C. J., *Healthy Attitudes Towards Love and Sex.* P. J. Kenedy & Sons, New York, 1964. pp. 40 to 43.
3. Schneiders, Alexander A., *Adolescents and the Challenge of Maturity.* Bruce, Milwaukee, 1965. p. 95.
4. Schneiders, Alexander A., *Personality Development and Adjustment in Adolescence.* Bruce, Milwaukee, 1960. p. 135.
5. Schlinder, John A., *How to Live 365 Days a Year.* Prentice-Hall, Englewood Cliffs, New Jersey, 1964. p. 151.
6. Haring, Bernard, *Shalom: Peace.* Farrar, Strauss & Giroux, New York, 1967. p. 198.
7. Lewis, C. S., *Mere Christianity.* The Macmillan Company, New York, 1960. p. 79.
8. McGinley, Phyllis, *The Province of the Heart.* The Viking Press, 1959. pp. 35 and 39.
9. Haring, Bernard, *op. cit.*
10. Evely, Louis, *We Dare to Say Our Father.* Herder & Herder, New York.
11. Duvall, Evelyn Mills, *Why Wait Till Marriage?* Association Press, New York, 1965.
12. Halleck, Seymour, "Sex and Mental Health on Campus."
13. Duvall, Evelyn Mills, *op. cit.*
14. Duvall, Evelyn Mills, *op. cit.*
15. Van Buren, Abigail, *Dear Teen-Ager.* Cardinal paperback edition, January 1961.
16. Mace, David, in *McCall's* magazine, August 1961.
17. *Life* magazine.
18. *A New Catechism.* Herder and Herder, New York, 1967. p. 410, 411.

19. Williams, Margery, *The Velveteen Rabbit.* Doubleday & Company, Inc., Garden City, New York. No date.
20. Quoted in the *New York Times,* December 17, 1963. p. 33.
21. Bronfenbrenner, Urie, "The Split Level Family," *The Saturday Review of Literature,* October 7, 1967.
22. West, Morris L., *The Devil's Advocate.* William Morrow & Company, New York, 1959. pp. 237-238.
23. Lewis, C. S., "We Have No Right To Happiness," the Curtis Publishing Company. First published in the *Saturday Evening Post,* issue of December 21-28, 1963.
24. Quoted in *Counseling the Catholic* by Hagmaier and Gleason. Sheed and Ward, New York, 1959. p. 101-102.
25. Halleck, Seymour, *op. cit.*
26. WHO Chronicle. Printed in Switzerland, 1965. April, 1965. Vol. 19, No. 4, pp. 146-147.
27. "About Syphilis and Gonorrhea." U.S. Department of Health, Education and Welfare. Health Information Series No. 84. U.S. Government Printing Office, 1964.
28. Bolt, Robert, *A Man For All Seasons.* Random House, New York, 1960. p. 132.